ATTENTION: ORGANIZATIONS AND CORPORATIONS

Island Entertainment Media Books may be purchased for educational, business, or sales promotional use. For information, please e-mail the Special Markets Dept. at IslandEntertainmentMedia@gmail.com

Holy Cow, Can You Believe That

Popeye Harnish

IEM TEXAS

Island Entertainment Media

IEM Texas

1001 N. Travis

Sherman, TX 75090

2015 Produced, Distributed, & Published by Island Entertainment Media

ISBN-13: 978-0692537503 (Island Entertainment Media)

ISBN-10: 0692537503

Printed in the United States of America

Visit Island Entertainment Media on the World Wide Web at www.IslandEntertainmentMedia.com

For appearances from the author, please contact
<u>IslandEntertainmentMedia@gmail.com</u> . Or visit
<u>www.iemTexas.com</u>.

Published, Produced, & Distributed by:

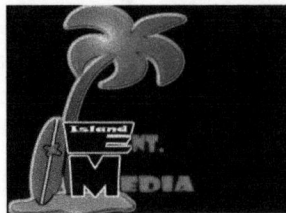

From the author of

Escape from the Southern Comfort Christian Society

Popeye Harnish

HOLY COW CAN YOU BELIEVE THAT

God Stories From The Back Of The Herd ~

www.popeyeharnish.com

A collection of God Stories and advice from Grandparents who have invested a lifetime in their children and grandchildren. Read their life-changing God Stories and experience the supernatural realm of a loving God.

Holy Cow Can You Believe That

By Popeye Harnish

Printed in the United States of America

ISBN-13: 978-0692537503 (Island Entertainment Media)

ISBN-10: 0692537503

Unless otherwise indicated, Bible quotations are taken from The King James Version: The New International Version. Copyright @ 973, 1978, 1984, 2011 by Biblica, Inc. Used by permission, All rights reserved worldwide; and The New Living Translation, Copyright @ 1996, 2004, 2007 by Tyndale House Foundation. Conversations The Message With Its Translator Eugene H. Peterson; NavPress. Used by permission Copyright 2007 by Eugene H. Peterson, Project Editor, Ken Gire.

Dedication

We dedicate this book to the sons and daughters of the Harnish family. They include present day children and grandchildren and now some great grandchildren who are scattered throughout Texas, New York, Virginia, and Oklahoma. They are:

Jim & Tammy Townsend

Chris & Jamelyn Rouze,

Jordon & Sonya Townsend, Harper

Rev Jay & Tracy Erickson, Nicholas, Emmalea Joy & Bryce

Rev Shawn & Julie Harnish, Taylor, Tyler, Zachary & Baylie

Chuck Parr, Brantlee, Shelby

Truston Parr, Charlie Rose, Madison, Tori & Quintin

Brian & Chanda Boss, Brendan, Christian & Zackary

Amanda Jeffries

May Father God be revealed on stage for the world to see his mighty works through the Back of The Herd.

Popeye Harnish

Back of the Herd
Hall of Fame Recipient: Myrna M Peterson

It is with great pleasure that we have selected Myrna M Peterson as our first recipient of the Back Of The Herd Hall of Fame inductee. Ms. Pete, to myself and hundreds of others, continues to have that captivating smile and that magical tone that only understands uplifting. If your paths have crossed with Ms. Pete in your kingdom walk, you have entered into a relationship engineered by Father God that will change you forever.

Of all the candidates for this award, Ms. Pete stands out because her connection with everybody is the same: she is totally invested in you at first sight and her understanding of God's love working through her gives you instant peace.

Day in and day out, your relationship with Ms. Pete will mesmerize you as you experience the love of God working through her regardless of where you are in your walk.

When I sat with Ms. Pete and asked her to edit my first book, **Escape from the Southern Comfort Christian Society**, little did I know that she would become the best Back of The Herd Sister I ever had. She loves me, she teaches me and she walks it out, regardless of my faults. I knew she was educated at Texas Wesleyan University and worked as a teacher for twenty-nine years at Pottsboro, but I did not know she never quit teaching. God just kept using Ms. Pete, day in and day out, to serve His plan for her; helping others.

Many months ago, I approached Ms. Pete about telling me more God Stories about her life, family and being my editor for **Holy Cow Can You Believe That.** She grabbed my arm and looked me straight in the eye and said, "You know I will, but first I am leaving for about a week and when I get back, we will get started."

I sat with her today in her room at the hospital and we talked. Both of us have been embattled with terminal illness and we share a special bond over that. We agreed that our connection was standing together daily on Father God's promises; we also agreed that we would not lean on our own understanding but in all ways we would trust God.

Ms. Pete has never left my mind during these authored works. She plays such an important part in every part of this book. It was Ms. Pete that Father God put in relationship with me to review its contents. Our sincere congratulations and thanks for who you are and all you do.

Update: Ms. Pete went to meet the Lord May 3, 2014 in the comfort of her home and family.

Popeye Harnish

Acknowledgments

Myra M. Peterson, Senior Editor for your time spent in correction, adjusting, and spiritual input to bring the God Stories of the Back Of The Herd into focus and reality.

Jon Erickson, Editor for those long hours of careful work to make the English language become compliant with writing rules and established patterns. For the work that nobody saw as you served Christ in this endeavor.

Pastor Duane Sheriff for preaching the truth about a living God, including sermons, CDs, and other teachings.

Pastor Terry Brown for answers of truth, support, knowledge, and wisdom while riding the roller coaster in the Kingdom walk. For taking the time to listen and give "real feedback." For prayers of faith and agreement.

JT & Debbie Wright for "overview reading," and content analysis.

To my gift from God, my wife Rhonda (my bride) (Saint Rhonda) (Nana) for saying "No, do it this way," and "Yes, that's so good, dear" and checking all my facts. Thanks.

Endorsements

I have known Popeye Jay for many years and he lives what he believes. This book is filled with wonderful stories that will make you laugh and cry. You will receive a lot of life lessons and Scripture applications, as well as great testimonies and insight. I especially was moved by "Matt's Story," as well as Popeye's own personal living testimony I encourage you to read it in one setting as I did with a cup of coffee and a lot of WOWs!"

Resident Pastor Terry Brown,

Victory Life Church, Sherman, Texas/Duane Sheriff Ministries.

In his book, "Holy Cow Can You Believe That," Popeye Harnish does a good job of helping us connect the dots between life's ups and downs and Gods ultimate desire to show us His unconditional love. The true life stories have very real applications and implications that reveal insights of God's grace for all of us. I believe every reader will find something of value in the stories shared in the pages of this book.

Lee Armstrong

Governing Elder and Associate Pastor / Victory Life Church

Table of Contents

Introduction

Several years ago, Pastor Pat Butcher preached a sermon at Victory Life Jubilee in Durant on the 'Back of the Herd." He correlated the ages of our congregation to the ages of a herd of cattle. At the age of 71 I'm certainly in the back of the herd. Most enter this section of the herd by age 62.

So, herein lies the God Stories from my brothers and sisters at the back of the herd. Each of us yearns to fulfill God's plan in our lives by sharing our story. We want our grandchildren to have an expanded reality, not just the television version. We want to help them skip over pitfalls that changes lives in less than two seconds. We want to put God Stories from the Bible into the God Stories of our lives so that they experience a rite of passage to live out a God-derived, God-sustained, and God-blessed life for themselves.

Psalms 116:9 "I walk before the Lord in the land of the living."

Lastly, we want them to understand "It's not about you, hot rod."

Disclaimer:

It is unprecedented and somewhat epoch-making for an author to make the following disclaimer prior to you reading the book. However, this book contains elements of fictional writing that have been used to illustrate a story within a story. The stories have added verisimilitude by supplying plausible backgrounds, locations, and characters.

The writing also includes its counterpart – the non-fiction style of giving the reader God Stories of credibility. I am not sure I totally qualify as an authority on Back of The Herd God Stories, but I have heard and collected many. This much I can stand on – I have actually explored firsthand the places and God Stories described. If the question "Why the mix and match of writing styles" comes up, its aim was solely to provide a reasonable solution to safety, and security for the folks I interviewed. Bearing one's soul in an interview over "kingdom walk storms" should not result in backlash to anyone.

Section 1

Behind Each Entrance is the Gateway to this God Story

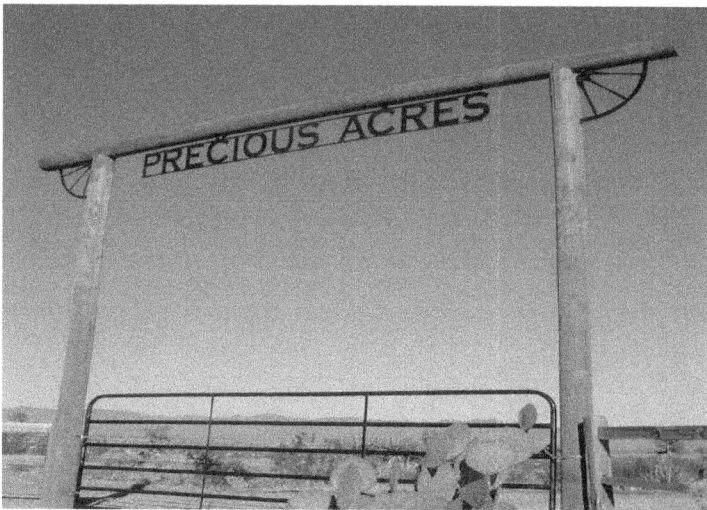

Popeye Harnish

Chapter 1
Ye should know the truth and the truth will make you free ~

Grandpa could not help but smile every time his daughter, Susan left her son Mark on the farm for a weekend visit. He loved the fact the boy would be underfoot and at the same time, he was concerned that Susan had forgotten her upbringing and whatever she was up to in the city certainly appeared to be a work of the enemy. Her divorce had been final just one year earlier in the month of May right before summer break. The very notion she left the farm after high school, traveled to the big city and got her University degree and disappeared from the landscape has always been a mixed bag of oats for Grandpa. Granted he always wanted the best for his daughter, just not her version. How could tons of cars and lots of noise from traffic jams ever replace the passing of one or two cars along their country road to town? How could living in an apartment complex full of next door folks you never met ever be better than having Mrs. Whitten down the south side of the road and Stone Phillips, his wife Nelly and their two border collies, Roller and Striker on the other side? Good neighbors are like old friends – it takes a long time to grow both. Susan is a high school counselor and at best, her father thought it was probably a safe place for her to work. Little did he understand about the racial tension of inner city schools.

Mark, on the other hand, was a five year old all boy version. Not only did he command a certain presence when he was in the room, but he had a way of making folks feel like everything they did for him was beyond belief super. Nobody could match Mark's ideas about his grandpa or his granny. Quick to line up with anything they said, he became, as you would expect, the apple of their eyes. The farm life was certainly Mark's idea of a super day – especially if he could help grandpa. To gather eggs, Mark would boldly step into the hen house and start telling each hen where and when to get out of his way so he could gather granny's eggs. Granny often smiled because her hens did not always move as quickly or orderly for her as they did for little Mark.

Granny had taken the time from day one to teach little Mark how to go about collecting eggs from the hen house. At first, she just let him carry the egg basket and she would show him as she instructed him on how to move the hen off her nest and get those large warm eggs into the basket. She showed him the proper way to carry an egg in his hand and gently place it in the open basket. Mark was, as we often put it, a quick learner. In less time than it takes to wash up and be ready for breakfast, little Mark was able to get all the eggs and not upset the hen house. Granny's joy of Mark's performance and ability could not outshine grandpa's since he was peeking around the corner watching the entire show. Mark would talk to the hens as if they were his brothers and sisters. Mark named them and never spoke to them unless he first called out their name. "Mary Jane, move over now and give me your eggs," he said. Mary Jane, a Rhode Island Red, side stepped out of the nest box and promptly plant herself on the pole above.

In church, Mark was always asking questions. In children's church, Jon told grandpa and granny that Mark had a vivid imagination. Jon said, "Mark told the class that he knows there are angels for real because they sometimes come to him at night and sing him to sleep." Mark also told the class about how Santa delivered presents to the Wise Men that night so baby Jesus could have gifts on His birthday. But the topper was Mark's belief that his grandpa could walk on water if he wanted to, just like Peter did. Grandpa and granny were somewhat concerned over Mark's boldness and his stories to his teacher and other classmates. Jon's final comment only added concern to the facts; "Some of the other kids believe him and everything he says."

Later that afternoon, when there was some quiet time after Sunday dinner, both grandparents asked Mark where he got the fact that Santa might have brought presents to the Wise Men the day Jesus was born. Mark did not blink – he just rolled his eyes back in his head and said, "Where else would the Wise Men get birthday presents? Wal-Mart is not open on Christmas day." A sigh of relief and a big smile gave both grandparents the opportunity to see just how easy it is for children to believe. Mark never took anything they said for granted. Mark was that serious child who loved life and took in everything with a ray of hope and belief that only comes from a child unhampered from a fallen worldview.

So what does this God Story about Mark and his grandparents tells us?

Children have no problems believing. They believe in a fat jolly man who wears a red suit and comes down the chimney to leave Christmas presents; who flies all the way around the world in one night in a sled pulled by reindeer. Children believe the Easter Bunny lays eggs; colored ones at that. When children see grandpa walk across the lane covered in water, they believe grandpa could walk on water just like Peter. When granny teaches them a song, "Jesus Loves the Little Children," kids like Mark think they are special and want to know this Jesus more.

They believe everything they encounter in their world before they ever see it. They will believe they are going to have a birthday party just as Jesus does at Christmas and wise men will bring them presents. They dream of what they can do with their toy drum set and how it will sound when they march to their beat. If you really want to witness joy, watch children right after they receive what they hoped they would receive. Squealing, shouting, clapping of hands, dancing, jumping jacks are all part of the celebration of truth. "I knew it, I knew it."

Children do not have to be taught to believe. God engineers all of us with the same truth; believe in Me. Nobody has to sit down with a child and explain belief, faith, trust, and promises. A child has all of them planted in his or her heart. It is their reality.

The truth is:

Grandpa and Granny would be quick to point out to you that your adult problems start with your loss of "belief." You used to believe and you did not even have to work at it. Think back to the days when "belief" was easy; now quit making it hard. Confess your sins to Jesus, be forgiven, and return to your journey down the kingdom road. Open those eyes to see and those ears to hear the word of God and fully believe as you did as a child. Ye shall know the truth and the truth shall set you free.

Popeye Harnish

Chapter 2

You have been taught your mess

PaPaw and MeMaw had raised four children in the same house, in the same town, from 1960 to early in the 1980's when the last girl, Janice Maria, left for college. John Edward, the oldest son had finished high school, joined the Air Force and now was married with two children living in Japan. There was no doubt the Armed Forces was his lifelong career choice. Harold Daniel, second oldest son also finished school, but decided to go to trade school to become a diesel mechanic. He lives just south of Tulsa and works for a local Drilling Company. Judy Lee was a cheerleader in high school, maintained a B average, and sang in the church choir on Sunday mornings. Three months prior to her high school graduation, she discovered she was with child. The child's father urged both his parents and Judy's parents to let them get married and promised he would love and take care of both Judy and the baby. Judy's husband Earl died in Viet Nam two months before their son was born.

The youngest child is the family wild child. There is four years between Judy and Cheryl in age. When Judy was a senior, Cheryl was just starting high school as a freshman. For years Cheryl watched her brothers and sister only to discover that deep inside she was jealous of the attention they got. With the brothers John and Harold it was not such a big deal; they at least moved off and she did not have to deal with them every day. However, with older sister Judy, the hot babe on campus, the cheerleader of all cheerleaders, she was constantly at war for attention.

Today I had the opportunity to sit down with the mother and talk with her about the choices her children made over the years. She started by telling me how her and her husband were certain they were doing everything correctly when the children were young. They attended church weekly, made sure the kids went to church summer camp, and knew for a fact all four had given their lives to Christ Jesus as their Lord and Savior. She also mentioned that all four had been water baptized before high school.

As the oldest boy John Edward entered high school my husband lost his job at a local factory. Perhaps the other children sensed that things were changing but John seemed to take it the hardest among the kids. John became very vocal about his forthcoming career choices way before his senior year in high school. He was all about joining the military so he would not have to worry about being laid off. I guess that notion served John well, because he has indeed lived a great life in the military and he has done extremely well for himself and his family. Today as I look back, I know for sure that we taught John job security was vital to keeping the family unit together. Strangely, we never taught him on purpose it just became a byproduct of my husband being laid off.

Harold graduated two years behind John. Harold was the quiet one in the clan. He tended to see his father as a source for tools, projects, and new adventures in the shop. He loved to take things apart and put things together, without the instructions. That in and of itself provided us with some humor along the way. Harold had a friend who would come by all the time named Jason. Jason's dad was a long distance truck driver and every once in a while he would invite both boys to travel with him on a short run over the weekend.

We never saw any reason not to allow it and Harold certainly wanted to go. Did Harold miss some church over those trips? Frankly, he did – but it did not appear to be a problem at the time. Harold never balked at going to church when he was home. Again, we did not realize it but Harold was learning missing church now and again was ok and God did not reach down and strike him dead over it. He also learned by our unwise choices that getting away from the house to ride in the truck was a way to escape anything he did not want to deal with. On the positive side, Jason's dad influenced Harold to not become a long distance driver and be away from home and his family but to take up diesel work in the shop. As Harold's last few weeks came into view in high school, he applied and accepted into Allied Tech School over in Mount Joy. Today Harold is shop foreman for a large Trucking Firm.

Then came Judy. Judy was the talker, the cute one, the flirt, and the "it's all about me" child. Being the first girl after two boys, I guess it was almost natural that my husband, my parents, his parents, and even myself paid more than the average amount of attention to little Ms. Princess. For the better part of her school years, she fit the "perfect little girl" that all parents dream of. She was popular, had looks, had good grades, was polite, and excelled in whatever she decided to do. Teachers, the preacher, and most of our friends always had nothing but glowing reports to talk about when it came to Judy.

I remember when it became evident that Judy and Earl were in a dating relationship that seemed to be getting too serious too soon. Earl was a polite well-spoken young man who attended our church with his parents. We had known the family for years and Earl certainly fit the mold as a good prospect for a son-in-law. Earl also played linebacker on the football team, and in their senior year, they achieved local greatness by winning the state title. I assume everyone thought Earl wanted to go on to college and play ball, but that was not the case. Earl like our other son had chosen a military life. Earl had worked for his uncle down at the cotton gin and over time had saved up enough money to buy himself a second-hand pickup truck. This could have been the beginning of the end. Earl started picking up Judy for a ride to school instead of her having to ride the school bus. At first, we did not think too much about it and Earl his polite manners led us to believe he also was a good driver.

The kids were to graduate from high school on May 18th. Somewhere around the end of February, I noticed that Judy seemed to tire easily. I checked her forehead for a fever; there was none, and asked her how she felt that morning. "I'm fine mom, really I'm fine," was her reply. A week later and now I am sensing that little Miss Judy is sick in the morning and she will not fess up. I approach her again thinking she got herself overly tired and just needs to rest some. First came the tears, then the uncontrollable sobbing, then the confession that she thought she might be with child. I calmly sat back down on the kitchen chair and quickly thought what my options were. I called our doctor's office and made an appointment for the next afternoon. That next twenty-four hours were nothing short of hell on earth. My husband did not take the news well at all. In fact, after twenty some years of marriage, that was the biggest verbal blowup I had ever seen from him. I knew enough to just stand back and let him vent his anger. Thank God, he has never hit a women or else little Miss Judy would be picking herself off the kitchen floor. As for Earl – the jury was still out and he may well be in the way of physical harm. Somehow we all survived the news. With counseling from our pastor and one or two meetings between Earl's parents and ourselves, everyone agreed the kids should get married right after high school graduation. The baby was due in early October and Earl left for boot camp on July 8th.

The second day of September, two military men stopped at our front door with news that Earl had died in a combat ambush three days prior. They gave us the details of when the body would arrive and what our options were. That news hit Judy so hard that our number one fear was she would deliver the baby before time. Ten days later, we buried young Earl in the church cemetery. I remember the pastor reading Psalm 23:4 "Yea, though I walk through the valley of the shadow of death, I will fear no evil: for thou art with me, thy rod and thy staff they comfort me." He closed the graveside service with, a verse from Proverbs 14, verse 32, "The wicked is driven away in his wickedness: but the righteous hath hope in his death." I remember trying to understand the hope that I heard.

Somehow, that day hope was as far removed as it has ever been. My heart was so broken for my daughter.

Almost two years to the day, we endured another family event that left all of us speechless. We sat in a court room and watched the judge sentence our youngest daughter to five years in the state penitentiary for possession of drugs with the intent to distribute. She had sold drugs to an undercover female officer while at a bar in the next town over in Denton County.

Cheryl was our needy child. When the selfishness started, I have never been sure of, but it was early on. At first, you just do not notice that the baby is getting increasingly demanding. How normal it is to cuddle the baby, how normal it is to give in because they are so cute. I also understand that Cheryl did not get this kind of attention from my husband and I. Cheryl worked everyone. She had more give me, give me, give me more than Janie More herself. By the time I was sick and tired, it was too late. Sick and tired got there because I did not get to where I needed to with Cheryl – her bottom end. In retrospect, I should have applied that discipline with love instead of pretending that giving her stuff was love. My parental love destroyed that child's ability to function on her own. Her selfish needs exploded way past, "please, pretty please," into demands. With the demands came the back talk and disrespect. With the little events getting larger and larger, we should not have been surprised at her getting involved in drugs.

Now after counseling, we understand with all our children, "we taught them." Today I have some valid advice for all parents. The Bible says in Proverbs 22:6 "Train up a child in the way he should go: and when he is old, he will not depart from it." Instruction are necessary – but without training, you have gained nothing.

So what does this God Story from two parents, now grandparents tells us?

One can raise four children in a godly home, with the same rules, guidance, knowledge, and opportunities and you will get four different results. The Bible says, "Train up a child;" not "Tell them what to do then wait and see if they do it." Our children often copy our behaviors, but you cannot expect them to learn fundamentals on their own. They do not come into this world looking to brush their teeth, take a bath, or change their clothes each day. They do come seeking our attention; seeking a relationship they can depend on; after all, they love you unconditionally.

One word of advice that both grandparents want you to know: starting today, it can be different. What you messed up on rearing your children is history; you cannot go back and change it. At best, you worked with what information you had at the time. Parents can never do better than what they are equipped to do. Your level of parental incompetence was directly connected to your level of understanding. Today you can offer your children advice about their children. Today you have the option of gaining more insight into God's plan for your family.

Do you still feel on the short side of parenting knowledge? We suggest Pastor Duane Sheriff's CD set on the family titled F300 Home Improvement III.

To learn more about what Jesus says; go to these Scriptures:

Proverbs 22:6 "Train up a child in the way he should go; and when he is old, he will not depart from it."

Proverbs 22:15 "Foolishness is bound in the heart of a child; but the rod of correction shall drive it far from him."

Proverbs 29:15 "The rod and reproof give wisdom: but a child left to himself bringeth his mother to shame."

Proverbs 13:24 "He that spareth his rod hateth his son: but he that loveth him chasteneth him betimes (early)."

Chapter 3
Grow up and get over it

The first words out of this grandmother's mouth came with a sigh as she wiped away a tear from the corner of her eye. I could tell that emotions were more evident in this interview and that words to tell the story would come with great pain. As she drew in another breath of air, she began to tell me how her ex-husband had not only physically, but mentally beat on her and in complete desperation, she had taken her two children and moved back to Texas completely empty-handed. She went on to say, "My story is not that different from many young mothers. Here I am – fifteen years later – watching my daughter play the victim role like the entire world owes her something; that perhaps is a little different."

She excused herself from the interview long enough to get the grandson by her side another glass of milk. I inquired about the boy and she told me that she had been taking care of him off and on for the last five years. I took him when Darla left town with a guy and left him with the babysitter. I took him when Darla did a year for possession. I took him when Darla could not find work and decided to go away to truck driving school. Honestly, I believe his only chance to grow up in a healthy home is for him to remain with me. I'm faced with the other problem that many grandmothers have these days. I don't have the cash to go to court to get custody and I don't have the ability to stop Darla from rushing in during one of her guilt trips and taking him away.

I decided now was as good a time to ask the hard question: "What do you think happened as you raised Darla? Has it always been a struggle?" "Without a doubt, the first six months back in Texas was more than a struggle," she said. "I stayed with an old girl friend from high school for the first two weeks." I did land a job at McDonald's within two days, but it didn't pay enough for me to get out on my own. My friend Janet and I had both been raised in the church and I went with her from day one when I moved in. I remember how safe it felt to go to Sunday morning services. But, once you leave the church, the real world is waiting just around the corner and that dose of reality isn't any fun. To my knowledge, there was not a shelter for women and because I wasn't doing drugs myself, there wasn't any program for me to go to for help. I did think about the Salvation Army, but their rules didn't allow you to move in long term, especially with two kids.

Like so many younger single moms, I let an older man talk me into living with him. Harold was eight years my senior and my shift boss at McDonald's. At first, things were ok, but as you can well imagine, living in sin out of wedlock was just another drama waiting to happen. Granted, I put a roof over my head and Darla's and Tommy's head. Granted, I got both of them into a school, and to a degree, things looked and acted normal.

I guess my first sign that this was not going to work started with Harold refusing to go to church with me and the kids. Back in the courting stages, he was all about it; but no sooner had we moved in, he backed out. Harold would have no part of church. In fact, most Sunday mornings, he was still hung over from drinking the night before. At first I thought Harold was just having a beer to relax; wrong. I honestly don't remember when Harold changed but it didn't take long; could have been as soon as three or four months. My first clue was Harold getting too much beer and wanting rougher than normal sex. Before long, that wasn't enough and his moods started to change even without the aid of beer.

I remember the day I was cleaning up a spill on the kitchen floor and Harold walked into the kitchen and went off like a crazy man. He started yelling and giving me all sorts of hell over the spill and how it cost him money and how I was disrespecting his house. And before I knew it, I was picking myself off the floor. That afternoon, I left with an ice bag over my swollen eye and vowed Harold would never hit me again. The sad part was both kids saw the whole event. I caught Janet just bawling. To get into a shelter for women, I had to take Darla and Tommy and move to another town close by. Finally, after getting another job, saving some money, and getting some help from the people at the shelter, I landed a small one-bedroom apartment we could afford. I used the public bus system to get to work and back. Thank goodness the kids were within walking distance of the school.

The next two years were certainly not glory to glory; they were struggle to struggle. If it wasn't one thing, it was something else. I do blame myself for having to leave the kids alone so much. Back then, they called them latchkey kids. There was not a YMCA or Boys and Girls club like today. It was just hang out at the school yard play ground across from our apartment or hang out in front of the apartment.

Next came the problems at school. Tommy was branded a bully and Darla won't do her homework. When the principal suspended Tommy for fighting, he was left home alone. The school's punishment was Tommy's delight. Then came the involvement in the gang. Tommy quickly took up with the locals and by the time he was fifteen, he was standing in front of a judge charged with possession with the intent to distribute. I had no money for a lawyer so the public defender cut a deal for Tommy and he got sent to the Texas Youth Commission for boys. Tommy was released and placed on parole. Within three months, he violated his parole and had new charges pending. Today Tommy is housed at TDC on a ten-year sentence. My heart has been broken so many times because I blame myself for what happened to Tommy. After years of counseling, I'm beginning to understand forgiveness and how to rid myself of condemnation. It's not easy being a mother.

Darla's attitude and behavior seemed to just elevate after Tommy was gone. She became verbally abusive towards me, very demanding, and I can't tell you the number of times she ran away from home. I think back to those days and I also have to admit there were times I was glad she had run away.

Today Darla is on her third marriage. Darla has never held down a job for more than three to four months. The sad part is Darla is smart; perhaps too smart for her own good. She lives in a world that is self-serving, is demanding, and is plagued with "It's their fault." I cannot remember her ever taking responsibility for any of her problems. She plays the blame game better than anyone I knew.

Currently, Darla is in counseling because CPS threatened to remove the child from the home. Like I said before, Darla would get to feeling guilty because I was taking care of my grandson and she would come and take him away. Her latest mistake was leaving him in the car while she ran into the Gas Station for a coke. A lady at the pumps called the police and when they arrived, they called CPS. Texas heat is no place for a child alone in a car.

As we speak, it's been almost four months that Darla has been going to counseling. I actually have to admit I'm seeing some positive changes. The biggest change was to get visitation with her son, she has to go to church supervised on Sunday mornings. This earns her the right to have other supervised visitations. I do believe the Lord is working in her life. I'm seeing a change in behavior and in attitude. Please understand that after all these years of embattlement, I'm not believing what I hear; I'm waiting for what I see on the behavior side. Where is the love, where is the caring, where is the idea of putting someone else in front of you and dropping the selfish moves? That's the fruit that I need to see.

I did get the chance, and the nerve to ask her the other day how things were going. Her comment shocked me. "Mom, I just needed to grow up and get over it." Really, I thought, that's a good thing; we'll see.

A day never goes by that I don't pray to Father God about my children; both of them.

I've learned to turn them over to Him. I've learned to trust in His word;   I lean on

James 1:17 that says, "Every good gift and every perfect gift is from above, and cometh down from the Father of lights, with whom is no variableness, neither shadow of turning." I believe that God is not finished with me or my children.

The miracle and blessing that God has given me is my children are still alive.

So, this God Story from one young grandmother tells us what?

Life's circumstances can bring about a reduced number of options without much notice.

There is a tendency for a rainstorm to turn into a hurricane in short notice; all one has to do is add wind.

Single mothers often find that the delicate balancing act of "day-to-day survival," reaches out to her children over time with far reaching ramifications that didn't seem to be in the picture at the time. Her survival choices often are less then desirable even to her; yet without the support network necessary, the enemy has a field day planting seeds of selfishness and greed in the children.

Children will always take the road to self-promotion one way or the other. A guilt-driven mother often tries to compensate for what she knows is not available to her children. It manifests itself by giving in to the demands of children. It displays its ugly head during timeframes that the single mother cannot fulfill normal family structure. Latchkey children begin to define themselves as victims and they develop "blame games," that fill in the gaps of negative feelings. When attention is an issue, the method to gain attention is not a factor. Children will act out to gain attention as quickly as acting good to gain attention.

A great church will be attentive to the needs of widows, single moms, and children in homes with only one parent. Mentors often emerge to help replace the missing father. Life Groups for single parents are put in place to develop alternative choices and to understand necessary relationships to maintain a balance.

In the end, children who develop and engage in anti-social behavior, crime and

burdensome reliance on mothers often find that they cannot function in society

because they lack the developmental skills necessary to just live. They become co-

dependent to the point of repeated failures.

The final "tough love" occurs when the single parent finally places positive restrictions on the unhealthy "help wanted," events of the past. They start with closing Mom's First

National Bank where loans were made without thought of repayment. They no longer allow the grown child to move back in until they can get it together. They quit doing for the child and point them towards solutions that can answer life's challengers.

In doing so, they endure the sights and sounds of a child who fails. They get to deal with the reality of how much damage can occur by being an "enabler." They return to Father God and hand the child back and pray that a mighty work will someday give the child the opportunity to live and grow as a healthy adult. They learn to pray the Word over their children. They learn to operate from a stance of "grace" without supporting the sin.

If this sounds like your circumstances and the shoe fits, wear it. Nothing short of giving your mess to Father God will do. Through the ups and downs, through the tears, our God is faithful and just. Stay the course and keep your eyes on God; He is your Savior and He loves you. Storms, and troubles will come but the joy will also come as you and your children each become all they can be in God's plan. This, too, shall pass; it's but for a season.

Here are the verses I turn to in times like this:

Deuteronomy 28:2 "All these blessings will come down on you and spread out beyond you because you have responded to the Voice of GOD, your God." The Message Bible

Matthew 6:8 "Don't fall for that nonsense. This is your Father you are dealing with, and

he knows better than you what you need." The Message Bible

Matthew 7:7 "Don't bargain with God. Be direct. Ask for what you need."

The Message Bible

Popeye Harnish

Chapter 4

Life ends as you know it in one second

Deuteronomy 21:20 "And they shall say unto the elders of his city, This our son is stubborn and rebellious, he will not obey our voice; he is a glutton, and a drunkard."

As a Parole Officer for the State of Texas, one of my jobs was to talk with contacts and references that the inmate list in their Parole Board package. We typically would do a home visit to the residence where the inmate was going to be after being released on parole. It was part of a pre-assessment. This then was the circumstances that first brought me into contact with Matt's story.

Nothing is sadder than parents and grandparents telling a story about how one of their sons lost his life, as he knew it, to one bad choice that occurred in less than two minutes. Life-changing decisions are born from sin and sometimes that sin looks as pure as the wind-driven snow. Here's their story about Matt.

The drive from the campus on the University of Texas in Austin to Corpus Christi is two hundred and seventeen miles and it takes about three hours and fourteen minutes if you stay within the speed limit. The date is May 19, 1969 and four young men are travelling south to the beach to celebrate their graduation from the University of Texas in Austin.

The commencement ceremony lasted about two hours so their departure time was late, sometime around seven pm.

What could be better than graduating from UT Austin after four years of struggle and study? The uncommon factor about these four boys is their backgrounds and their normal behavior during their college years. By and large, they were not part of the social action on campus – they didn't party hard, they didn't join the frat scene, and they would more commonly be called geek freaks if they were on campus today.

By the same token, all four young men had dreams, fantasies, and thoughts about what it would be like to become part of the in crowd. During their entire four years at UT Austin, they never once ventured down to the yearly party bash on the beaches of south Texas. No girls gone wild nights, no crazy drinking bouts, and certainly no sex on the beach.

Somewhere in their brains, their parents and perhaps even more so, the grandparents, had fixed a "warning sign," about the results of all that party life on campus stuff. It came with warnings that they were not being sent to the University to party; no, they were commissioned to be successful and make their family proud. Lastly, the cost of going to school was a great burden on the family and not to be taken lightly by the boys.

Church was also a part of all four of the boys' backgrounds. Two if we recall correctly were Baptist, one Methodist, and the other Catholic. We could be wrong about those denominations, but you get our point.

On the trip down to the beach, the boys decided it would be neat to start the party early so they stopped somewhere between Austin and San Antonio to pick up one bottle of wine. The sheer embarrassment of buying booze was so out of character for them that they elected to send in the Catholic boy to do the dirty work. As they drove into the darkness of night, they passed the wine bottle around until it was gone. Without experience in drinking, it didn't take but a few ounces of wine to make all four of them happy campers. Finally they reached their hotel and immediately went to bed because they all felt tipsy. So much for all night fun and the anticipated party.

The next morning, they woke up and realized they were somewhat hung over and each had experienced a headache. Breakfast; and coffee; that would be the cure they thought they needed. Being a straight bunch of good boys, they each took the time to shower and get on clean clothes. Matt felt thirsty and drank at least two glasses of water after he brushed his teeth. After showers and fresh clothes, they all piled down the stairs into the Volkswagen van that belonged to Matt and started to a restaurant for breakfast.

Although Matt realized he was hung over, it never dawned on him that his driving would be impaired. Matt himself declared that his notion of drunk driving would have been from the night before – not the next day. Certainly, his blood alcohol levels would have subsided after that much time. The truth is, Matt was correct, he was not drunk or driving drunk that next morning.

As Matt pulled out onto the street the morning, sun hit him right in the face. Before he could get the visor down, he realized he was also feeling woozy. Matt's first memory after that was waking up with tubes everywhere in his body. The next few weeks were spent trying to stay alive. Finally, he was taken from ICU and put in his private room. As he began to respond to his parents and grandparents, he realized that something was very, very wrong.

The writer's interview with Matt ~

By the time I met Matt, I had done hundreds of parole officer interviews for returning inmates who were now living in the free world, but living under the guidance and rules of being on parole.

The standard questions and the rule review was more than boring. Somehow the majority of returning inmates all shared the same or very similar backgrounds, crime activity, and it was not uncommon to place each one into a predetermined square hole almost without thought and assume they were just going to be one more person to chase down.

Typically, they tell you everything you ever wanted to hear during that first interview and by their account, you will never have any problems with them. They all had learned their lessons in life, had done their time, and were ready to lead productive lives. I could only wish that had been true. By the time I added Matt to my caseload, I had over 128 drug dealers, but not Matt. Matt's case was so unusual that I didn't have a single other case to compare it with.

After all the standard fill in the blank answers, I started to makes notes on his version of what happened. My first question was, "Can you tell me about what happened that Sunday morning?" Matt looked at me with a blank stare and said, "I wish I could remember. The first time I was awake enough to see where I was, I saw the newspaper next to my bed with the headlines and picture of the head-on crash."

All three of his friends from college were dead from the accident and he killed five other family members on their way to church. They determined that both vans hit head on at approximately forty five miles per hour. Matt wasn't even up to the highway speed when it happened. The oncoming van was preparing to make a left turn; Matt somehow crossed over the line just far enough to hit them head-on.

After months in jail awaiting a trial, Matt finally had his day in court. Tearfully he heard the jury's final words: guilty. Matt had been convicted on multiple counts of vehicular manslaughter. His sentence was twenty years to life. Life as he had known it ended for the next twenty years and then some. You have to understand that your first few times in front of the State Parole Board usually means you will be turned down for parole. Add those years and the perfect inmate will out do his first release date. His recollections and accounts of what happened to him in prison are so graphic that I choose to skip over the details. I think it can best be described as being a "pawn." Whenever, whereever, and any time from anybody Matt was victimized.

Somehow Matt found hope in his faith in Jesus Christ. Every opportunity he got to read or study, that activity took away the fear associated with just being there. Time was his number one mental killer. For days and weeks on end, he would devise ways to cope with the idea of being over forty or fifty or perhaps sixty years old if he ever got out. It became a day-to-day struggle and only those few moments with Father God cleared the air. What hope was there for me, I had nothing to look forward to except a life of ruin.

My first interview with Matt that I just described was during the time I was a Parole Officer in Dallas, Texas. I had switched human resource careers because I was tired of dealing with drug addicts in rehab settings. As I listened to his story, I was floored. My heart just sank as I listen to the circumstances that lead to that fatal day. That was Matt's first drink he had ever had on that night before he drove to Corpus Christi. "My decision to drink, not get enough sleep, and then plunge out onto the highway when I could not see well was the biggest "piece of stupid" I had ever committed in my life," he said.

That was the first time I realized just how much devastation could occur over one stupid choice. Here was this kid well on his way to fame and fortune – and it all disappeared in two minutes over one piece of stupid. Matt was a model case from the get go. He continued to attend his AA meetings, was on time for all his appointments, and never was late on his parole fees. Over time, I found out he was finishing up his degree in law. When he became a lawyer, he could not work as an attorney because of his convictions. Matt choose to help people at a free law clinic for the poor and disadvantaged people. Matt also goes into the schools and talks to kids about drinking and drugs. Before I left my position as a Parole Officer, I got Matt's case moved over to reporting once a year.

So, this story from one set of grandparents tells us what?

God's plan for Matt's life was certainly unknown to Matt or his family. Nothing ever came close to Matt seeing himself in prison. Matt regarded himself as one who obeyed the laws of the land, one who was conservative, and one who always leaned into the safe side of life.

Matt's crime didn't just ruin Matt's life. Matt's crime had far-reaching ramifications that changed his parents and our lives forever. We all suffered a different kind of pain and sorrow over the loss of a son and grandson in our daily lives. The brightest days when visitation occurred were also the blackest days for everyone involved.

As Matt's grandparents, we grieved over his circumstances that would place our grandson in prison for over twenty years. We both remember Matt telling us that he should have never listened to that little voice that said, "Go ahead, Matt – you deserve to have a little fun. Nothing bad can come from one drink."

We're not sure what we can say to other young people about how the devil tempts and comes to steal, kill, and destroy lives. We can tell them that Matt never got up that morning and decided today would be a good day to kill three of his friends and kill five members of another family. Matt never wanted anything in life after college more than to return home be successful in business, marry, have a family, and go to church. Matt would have been our fourth generation to do just that.

Matt has escaped the jaws that so tightly fit around his life and today he serves both God and mankind. He's living proof of our DNA; Love God, Love People, and serve Both. Matt can't change his history or take it all back. Matt does understand that God forgives and God loves him. Only through Christ could Matt become a successful God Story.

I can still hear the grandfather's parting words; "You kids can blow this off all you want to – but remember one thing. It only takes one bad decision, one bad choice – and in less than two minutes, you find your life completely gone. God will hear you if you ask for forgiveness, but the man at the big house will never hear you." Remember this verse from Matthew chapter six; verse eight "Be not ye therefore like unto them; for your Father knoweth what things ye have need of before ye ask him."

Popeye Harnish

Chapter 5
Let God Find Your Husband

Genesis 2:24 "Therefore shall a man leave his father and mother, and shall cleave unto his wife; and they shall be one flesh."

I guess any time one can remember their high school years from late 1958 up to and including 1962, you have dated yourself as a member of the back of the herd. Today I have been married to Ray for fifty-one years and we have two sons, five granddaughters and a full life. But the real story started when I was a teenager in high school.

Typical of the time period, teenagers, including me, had little or no access to today's social media such as Facebook, Twitter or Pinterest. We had no computers, telephones and some, for many years, went without television. Radio, yes, church yes, and our local newspaper that carried everything from weddings to funerals. Typically they would have a few headline news items of national interest, none of which I ever read. To a degree, we lived in our village vacuum. Located in upstate New York, we were the natives of the five finger lakes sections and dairy after dairy of milking cows. Inside our town, we had the famous Ingersoll Rand and over the other side of Riverside, we had Corning Glass Works. That was our claim to fame. No, we were not any part of the New York City scene that you normally think of when someone says they are from New York.

Without a doubt, we did have a community with many diverse backgrounds and cultures. We had plenty of Italians, Polish, Greeks, Germans, some Jews, French and the rest were a combination of blended European backgrounds, at large. Some of the more predominate cultures in today's world never darkened our door. We had no African Americans, or Mexican Americans or Asians that I remember. As the saying used to go, we were a pretty good collection of WASPs (white Angelo Saxon Protestants) and Catholics. It was clear that we were a hard-working people with strong morals, and beliefs.

So, quickly it becomes evident that our diverse backgrounds offered each of us some different ethic practices and spiritual upbringings. The one tie that binds was being an American. Most of our grandparents had come to America and even some of our parents came from the old country. Pledge to the flag and prayer were not banned in our schools. We spoke English correctly, and wrote it precisely. Rules were rules and, for the most part, we paid attention to them based on the negative reinforcement measures that were part of our schooling at that time. I would have to say for the most part, we were a church going community. We had all your standards in place, Catholic, Methodist, Baptist, Assembly of God and some faith based works that were not tied into a particular denomination. If church wasn't your thing, we had Knights of Columbus or the Moose and Elks lodges to hang out at. The flip side was we also had a reputation of having the most bars in any one given block in any city on Market Street in Corning. They used to say the most seasoned sailor could never take one drink at the first bar and see the end of the street if he continued from bar to bar. But once again, our parents did a great job of keeping us out of those places.

I guess now at my age, I'm seeing God and His plans for my life being formed way before I realized what was going on. The core values that I got from going to Sunday School, Youth groups, and church had made an impact even in areas that I didn't recognize. Certainly I was learning from my parents, my school, and even some unwanted lessons from my peers. I, like most, grew up with incoming messages from all four areas. They did, however, have one common goal – and that was to teach me that they were right. They, in and of themselves, could point me in the right direction to not only do well in school, but also in life.

That left one part out of the "original picture" – me! I had only limited access to define who I was and what I was going to be. What I did have was "good girl manners and a good reputation." I recently looked in one of my old year books and realized that there were forty three girls in our high school class and sixty seven boys. With closure coming to an end in my Senior year, I was well on my way to being confused as to which path to take in life. Back then, choices to a degree were limited. Certainly the kids from affluent backgrounds and homes were pre-destined to attend the college of their parents' choice; especially if they had the grades. Many sought a suitable mate for life and aimed at becoming a successful domestic engineer. Others wandered aimlessly working some counter as a waitress in a local dinner or clerking at some local store.

I found myself behind the counter washing dishes at the Grove Diner over in Erwin across the river. Now I won't describe myself as lonely or even in a panic to have a boyfriend, let alone a husband. What I did have was three older brothers. As you may guess, with three older brothers, other boys would show up at the house and indeed, one fellow named Ray did. Being a country girl from a large family gives one the ability to survive most anything, including boys. Since these three brothers of mine were not part of the local angel flock, they somehow adopted the policy that they were the guardians over baby sister – that would be me.

The first night Ray came to the house, we were in the middle of playing tables games. Can you image that? A family that actually didn't watch TV 24/7 and played table games? I sort of liked Ray from the beginning, but he was interested in another girl who lived down the road. As time would have it, Ray became more of a fixture around the table.

Now, dad was a story all in himself. Dad didn't approve of boys for me and he knew that two had eyes on his daughter. As I was about to finish my duties at the diner that night, I glanced out the front diner window and saw that no one from my family was there to pick me up.

What I did see was Vet and Ray; the two suitors that daddy didn't like. At first, I think I felt some panic; who to choose? Being the sensible type, I waited to see if this entire deal would work itself out. Again, I peeked outside the window and saw Vet driving off. My hunch was correct – this had worked itself out all by itself. When I went to Ray's car, he told me that he'd assured Vet that he was here to pick me up; enough said. Indeed the work of my dad's hands. I'm also pretty sure daddy always got a kick out of sending both of those boys to the diner at the same time that night.

I never heard from Vet again and with him in college, I just let it go. Ray, on the other hand, just never gave up on me. Eventually I did see the good in him. But after living with Ray all these years, I am sure there was more to that story then just telling Vet he was there to pick me up. Not saying, my Ray would ever lie – he says, "It is just his excuse to avoid the truth."

To this day, I believe God had his hand in my marriage and my decision to marry Ray. I surely wasn't mature enough at that time to make the decision; it would have only been out of selfish reasons. As for the other girl that Ray was first interested in, she died almost ten years ago from a bad heart and Parkinson Disease. Ray and I often talk about what our lives would have been like if God hadn't put us together.

In these later years. Ray has gone through multiple illnesses and it's been the toughest of all tough things in our marriage. We are always so thankful for every minute, every hour, and every day that God gives us as a couple and family. Our blessings never stop and only through God's choice of a husband have I had the privilege of living such a blessed life.

For all you folks in the front of the herd, please don't rush and make choices without God in your life. Be all you can be in God's plan, so when He chooses your mate for life, you'll be ready to join in His union, His design, a family.

I do want to tell you one more tidbit of information about Ray. Back in high school, my friend Virginia and I were waiting for my dad to come pick us up after the wrestling matches. Along came Ray and his friend Bill. I guess the devil had ahold of Ray that night, because he grabbed my mittens and threw them up on the roof of the Post Office. Being the country girl that I was, I threatened him with his life if he didn't get them down. At that very moment, God's choice for my husband for life was a total jerk in my eyes.

Do keep your eyes on God and expect the unexpected.

Writer's notes: The wonderful lady was a classmate of mine in high school. Today she's a grandmother, wife, and a handy little writer herself. She always posts inspirational messages on her Facebook page and those who are closest to her see her as "this little light of mine." God bless you and your entire family for your faithfulness to our DNA: Love God, Love People, and Serve Both.

Chapter 6

Life in the wagon

Galatians 4:7 ~ "Doesn't that privilege of intimate conversation with God make it plain that you are not a slave, but a child? And if you are a child, you're also an heir, with complete access to the inheritance." The Message Bible

By 1947, our boys were back home from the war and everyone was well settled back into jobs and family life. Our 33rd US President was Harry Truman. In the news, Jackie Robinson becomes the first black in Major League baseball and Richard Button won the US Men's Figure Skating Championship. In Certralia IL, a coal mine explosion claimed 111 lives and over in the coalfields of southwestern West Virginia, a mother gave birth to her 7th child; a blond, blue eyed baby boy. By 1952, this baby boy was one of nine children in a family that could not keep up with the wages a coal miner made. Desperate to keep things afloat, the mother worked in a local café mornings to help get breakfast served.

The oldest girl kept the little ones in line while mother was gone and she made sure they got dressed and to the table for breakfast made mostly of gravy and sometimes cream of wheat.

On a sunny spring day, just like any other spring afternoon, the father came in from the coal mine to find his wife had disappeared. Fearful that something had happened to her he rushed over to the café and inquired about her whereabouts. Someone said they saw her leave with that trucker from across the mountain. Later that next day, all nine kids were loaded in the beat up old family station wagon and down the road they went looking for mommy.

Relentlessly in pursuit of his wife, the father drove from town to town searching in vain for her. When I talked to John, he doesn't recall how long they looked for his mom. What John remembers is the day his dad backed the station wagon up to the welfare office door and took all the kids out and lined them up. Without a word, he got back into his station wagon and drove away – never to be seen or heard from again.

Adoption was not a very popular activity in 1952. Most families had plenty of kids of their own and needing or taking in one or two more simply was out of the question. The only viable alternative for a child that was displaced was foster homes. A few loving, caring homes took in kids under the foster care program.

At first, John didn't think he'd ever have a real home. Today he cannot describe how devastated he was as a child; those memories have been locked out and put away forever. What John does remember is a young couple coming in and taking him home. His new foster home had an older boy in it and a younger sister and, even with everyone trying to make him feel at home, he was still scared it would end at any time.

One thing for sure was totally different about this foster home. Here, everyone went to Church – and to John, it seemed like that's all they did. Sunday morning church, Sunday night church, and Wednesday night church. Then every so often, they would go to the mission downtown and have church. About one year after he first moved in, they told John he was going to be adopted as their son.

Fast forward a few years and it became evident that church was where his adopted father was the pastor. By the age of twelve, he remembers being saved during an altar call at the church's youth camp. A few weeks later, he was baptized by his adopted father in the lake at the youth camp.

During all the rest of his teenage years, prior to leaving for the armed forces, he lived with the Word being preached daily – morning, noon, and night. He never entered into any sports in high school, had no particular hobby, and only in his senior year did he become attracted to playing pool. This one activity was hidden from his father because he knew he would not approve of playing pool in a pool hall.

Because the church and his adopted father were in the sin management business, John struggled to rise up to their high expectations. The exchanges between father and son grew to be more battle oriented By the time his senior year rolled around, John was bound and determined to join the armed forces. In fact, he did leave home right after high school and joined, not just the service, but Special Forces.

Today many Viet Nam veterans have never talked about their duty tours in Nam; John is one of those. During our interview, I asked about his thoughts concerning his adopted parents. His reply was he was grateful because they supplied food, clothing and a warm place to sleep. Nothing was said about spiritual growth or feelings of personal love.

When John returned from his tours overseas, he went home to his adopted family, only to find they had moved to another state and another church without ever telling him. No forwarding address; nothing. In John's mind, nothing had ever changed. The scars of youth remained intact after all those years. In his attempt to find a place of rest and peace, he ended up moving to Europe, where he traveled for the next two years with a backpack and small change from jobs along the way.

Eventually, he moved back to the States and settled on the Gulf in the heart of the south. He married a nurse who, after seven years of marriage, left him for the doctor she was working for and John never looked back. They did not have children.

For years, he was invited to attend various churches and he refused because of his deeply engrained ideas of what would occur if he started going there; eventual rejection and more pain and hurt. Yet the word of God had settled in his heart as a child to the point where reading the Bible became normal. Perhaps one of John's strongest suits is his knowledge about the Bible; from front to back I do know that John developed a relationship with a pastor and church online for years. He sent in his tithe and studied the Word. John's not a big talker and it's still hard for him to trust anyone. I've been in church with him once or twice, but it's not John's regular worship mode. John's relationship with Father God isn't mine and there is no Hollywood feel good story to end his God Story.

What I did get after the interview was a quiet miracle that God sometimes imparts to certain people. When John loves people and serves people, he doesn't let anybody know. The Bible says don't let your left hand know what your right hand is doing when it comes to good works; that's the John that I know. He loves God, Loves people, and serves both in a unique way.

Not all God Stories end with a bang. Some remain quiet in a soft still voice that says, "Well done, good and faithful servant."

Chapter 7
Old Eugene – my hero

This chapter relates parts of Eugene H Peterson's memoirs from his published book, The Pastor. His experiences, his insight, his God Stories bring about what Christianity Today called; a subtle manifesto of hope for our time.

Eugene H. Peterson, author of The Message Bible, a best - selling translation of the Bible, is Professor Emeritus of Spiritual Theology at Regent College, British Columbia, and the author of over thirty books. He and his wife, Jan, live in Montana.

So I'll pose the question that I think is already in your head, "Why would Popeye share his kingdom walk problems with stories that he read in Eugene H Peterson's book; The Pastor? And what benefit should we children, we grandchildren, and you the reader get?"

The answer is; "My ability to have life answers that are founded both in earth reality God Stories and Bible God Stories." I ask you ~ "what good is a grandfather, who is a Christian author, who doesn't even have the answers to all his lifelong problems that he wants us to avoid?"

I needed Peterson's insight, his wit, his revelations about things in the church that just flat confused me. Mostly, I needed a Bible I could read that made sense to me; something where I really did understand the words used, thus producing a real knowledge base capable of implementation today, tomorrow and next week.

I'm reminded of what Pastor Jacob Sheriff, my pastor at Victory Life Sherman said to me after our discussion about tying into Pastor Eugene Peterson's world of understanding and knowledge; and I quote Pastor Jacob's email reply to me:

"Merry Christmas to your family as well. I warn you though, once you tread down the path Eugene Peterson lays out, it is hard to come back. You just might not see the world the same again; which is great for you, but can be difficult to get others to see what you now see. I have a deep-seated appreciation for what he has done for me and how I view the Church, the Faith, and life in general. He is a precious gift to the Body of Christ, and I am thankful to have discovered him. Good luck to you as you dive into the thoughts of a great man of God."

Jacob

I knew for sure I didn't need another sixty plus years of God talk doctrine that emerged from the King James Version like a foreign language. When the preachers in my life quoted scripture or cited great revelations from the KJV, I often thought they were faking it till they made it. If they got loud enough, or threw up enough hand signals, somehow you'd believe they had it all figured out.

Now before you throw me under the bus for being "judgmental," let me say I do believe every word in the Bible; my issues of connection have always been centered over being able to connect the God Stories in the Bible to the God Stories of my everyday life.

Lesson One ~ seeking knowledge that works day by day

In Chapter one, Montana, Pastor Peterson gave me my first look at the issues surrounding my seeking knowledge that would work for me on a day by day schedule; and I quote:

"I was acquiring a sacred imagination strong enough to reject and resist the relentlessly secularized and ghettoized one-dimensional caricature that assigned American pastors to jobs in a workplace that markets religion."

The world of church, the world of God in your life, was changing. As I reached my early adulthood and withdrew from the church I returned from the Vietnam Era trip to a new church that confused me even further. Now I was having this confused experience of seeing pastors and churches engage in competition with one another for their share of the church market. New buildings, new programs, new ideas and now a larger than ever staff that had more college degrees in more subjects than you could count on one hand. There was the Senior Pastor of course, the Music Pastor, the Youth Pastor, the Media Pastor, and the Organizational Pastor, just to list a few. This corporate team of "pastors," were dynamic, fairly young, and full of self. I was always sure they would have their own television show any week now.

Frankly, I didn't want anything to do with it. Certainly I didn't sense that I could measure up to the greatest of their kingdom walk. The days of pastors being shepherds to the flock was disappearing in the massive influx of "more people." It was all about numbers; so and so church is growing, look at the parking lot, count the members.

Meanwhile, I'm searching for a meaningful relationship with God to help me get through life in general. I had storm after storm come, but the devil was often more interesting as an escape than going to Jesus with my problems. Society had changed so much from the short period of time I served in the US Navy that even on my arrival at the college gate, my first day was nothing short of a new war. Now the enemy was the kid down the street (that did not serve his country) and all his buddies and my peers. By the time I returned from military service, I was at least four years older than these college kids.

I was called out as a pig, a killer of children, because I engaged in the Viet Nam war. I had signs thrust in my face and I was so shocked I didn't even react. Later that first day, my veteran counselor told me to avoid the protest and watch my back because protestors would attack, as sure as the enemy did. The long and short of this story is I never talked about Viet Nam or being in the Navy for the next thirty years. Five years ago, an old Navy buddy tracked me down and told my wife that he wanted to talk to me because I had saved his life when we were in the service. Only then did I admit to being a sailor.

Back to church ~ my history does point to church hopping. I tried a combo church; Mennonite & AG folks, I tried Church of Christ, I tried a local Community Faith church, and I tried enough different kinds of Baptist churches till I was very, very confused.

Popeye Harnish

Lesson Two ~ Seeking answers outside of the church

The years spun by and I injected several college degrees into my brain, thinking the answers to life might be within that framework. I studied Sociology, Social Work, Human Services, Animal Science and lastly World Religion, my minor at the University of Texas Arlington. It was not. School was useful for knowledge and getting a career started, but it always fell short of another higher degree. Perhaps two Masters and a PhD would do the trick; not.

What I found in Pastor Peterson's book was the unknown answer was always there, but I just missed it. His discovery of the "sacred landscapes in the mountains of Montana that provide the material conditions for preserving his story he says; and I quote: "It has provided a stable location in space and time to give prayerful, meditative, discerning attention to the ways in which my life is being written into the comprehensive salvation story. It is the Holy Grounds from which the invisibilities of Father, Son, and Holy Spirit form a believing imagination where the "inside is larger than the outside."

This opens up my world and gives me new insight into God being with me when I lived alone on a farm high on the mountain over Bath, in upstate New York. I was embracing loneliness, emptiness, and doing battle with the winter elements like a mountain man. Wood burning stoves provided heat and a place to cook food; no hot water, and to boot, Mother Nature controlled the electric switch: on and off, on and off. Living on a mountain road that often as not was closed with high piles of snow blocking any coming and going. I once delivered Christmas presents with a horse and sled. Actually, that was pretty cool.

Now my rear view mirror is showing me the steps and places that Father God brought me through to allow me to serve Him today. I never was alone; just lonely.

Lesson Three ~ Learn to be a Christian

Pastor Peterson also turned on another light in my life. I'm fairly sure I've spent a large part of my life trying to learn to be a Christian. I was to say the least, a successful failure. I, like most of you, have never been able to measure up to the church standards. The more the church changed, the further away I was driven. Nobody would ever be able to measure up to that large pastoral staff of PhDs.

Pastor Peterson took this stance; and I quote: "I had only the vaguest of ideas of why I was there and certainly nothing that I would recognize as a pastoral vocation. I didn't know it at the time, but what I absorbed in my subconscious, which eventually surfaced years later, was a developing conviction that the most effective strategy for change, for revolution ~ at least on the large scale that the kingdom of God involves ~ comes from a minority working from the margins."

There was my answer to involvement with God and involvement with the church. All God was interested in was just "me." It wasn't about getting on staff or running alongside the Senior Pastor and his motley crew. This was about me, the minority servant, working from the margins of my inexperience. Here my Senior Pastor's words, Pastor Duane Sheriff, rang out loud and clear; and I quote, "God is looking for available, not capable. God will work in you to get through you and always provide exactly what's needed for His purpose and plan for your life."

That in combination set me free to serve my Lord and Savior. Father God had a purpose for me to be a Care Pastor, a Christian writer, a teacher, and to disciple others. Father God also wanted me to be a steward over His company that does construction for handicapped needs: Above Access. I like to translate Pastor Peterson's words into mine; "I had no idea then of how my years of study, work and community would be worked out vocationally as a Care Pastor, Writer, Teacher, Discipleship Man, and steward of His construction company." Additionally, each and every place I lived and each and every job I held combined to make me what I am today. Truthfully, I never wanted to be in ministry; I spent my life doing it for the money.

This disassembled Christian, not serving God life, attempted to keep the puzzle together over and over. I like the fact that Pastor Peterson took experiences on Mother Earth and tried to use them to support what I heard at church or what the preacher was trying to teach me.

Pastor Peterson talks about his time in his dad's butcher shop and his years of learning that trade. Then he recalls the new pastor that preached Sunday after Sunday out of Leviticus and quickly discovered this man knew nothing about killing animals. And I quote from page 38 ~ "And through we never butchered goats, the rich sensuality of Hebrew worship was reproduced daily in our workplace. It never occurred to me that the world of worship was tidy and sedate. Our pastor had it all figured out on paper, but I knew it wasn't like that at all. I couldn't help but wonder how much he knew about sin and forgiveness. He certainly knew nothing about animal sacrifices. Sacrifice was messy: blood sloshing on the floor, gutting the creatures and gathering up the entrails in buckets, skinning the animals, salting down the hides. And in the summertime, the flies ~ flies everywhere."

In the end, it would be years before someone like Pastor Duane Sheriff stood up in front of the congregation and told me (he also included all of those other folks in the service) I was an "are not." I "are not," smart enough, special enough, tough enough, and on and on he went, to provide me with a clear understanding that I had spent years looking in all the wrong places and to all the wrong people.

He set the tone for God to be the center of the way I was going to walk my kingdom walk; not me. Wrong thinking, inappropriate, fear driven, anxious leaping attempts would only stop me and distract me from looking at Father God. My job was to seek what God's purpose and plan for my life today was going to be. My focus had to be on Father God so that I could carry out His command to go and disciple and guide others to find that hourly, daily, weekly rhythm that would get God into my very being. At Care Group and at church, I was learning to stay in touch with individuals in need and in despair. I would pound their names into my head, knowing I'd never forget their faces. I'd learn to pray with them, read the Word with them, and redirect their questions back to Bible answers. I helped them connect their God Stories with the Bible God Stories.

Later, after being faithful in little, Father God started to add to my daily service to God. The book came first after the baptism of the Holy Spirit, then the website and the Word Press daily blog. Care Groups, hospital visits, and going out to bless someone needing a ramp. One mission has been to give away as many Psalms 91 books as possible that Peggy Joyce Ruth wrote. Today we have a Life Group called "Bookies," and those members have joined us in trips to VA hospitals and clinics to distribute Psalms 91 Military books and to pray and witness. What Pastor Peterson calls his awareness of congregation as a pastor became my awareness of being a servant with the flock that cross our pastures.

Lesson Four ~ The seduction of culture and religion

Leftover guilt and condemnation has resulted from some normal activity as an adopted PK (preacher's kid) child. At the time, I never gave it much thought. Certainly as a young boy, I was so happy to be out of that Catholic orphanage and in the home of good parents that I didn't care they were ex-Mennonites turned Baptist. My focus was on dry, warm clean clothes and food in the belly. That alone was enough to be happy about; or so I thought.

Pastor Peterson in his book talks about the year that his mother discovered the prophecy of Jeremiah and those very Bible verses ended up removing the family tradition of having a Christmas tree. And I quote from page 50 ~ "Thus says the Lord: "Learn not the way of the nations, nor be dismayed at the signs of the heavens because the nations are dismayed at them, for the customs of the peoples are false. A tree from the forest is cut down, and worked with an axe by the hands of a craftsman. Men deck it with silver and gold; they fasten it with hammer and nails so that it cannot move."

That was the end of the Christmas tree in Peterson's house. Pastor Peterson's mother, who was a women of strong belief decided that the Holy Spirit had targeted our American

Christmas in this passage. Every detail fit the American home activity.

Years later, Pastor Peterson said, "My mother's "No tree this year, brother, just Jesus," accompanied by my uncle's "damn, damn, damn" lay dormant in me for years, but in time it developed into practiced pastoral discernments ~ Jesus without tinsel ~ as I daily face the seductions of culture-religion."

In my world, it was the "one present, one fireplace stocking," Christmas that we had as growing children. We did indeed have a Christmas tree that we went into the woods and chopped down for free. We did indeed have a red bowl with green legs that held water to keep it upright and alive. All our Christmas trees were pine so all the needles fell off in the first five days. One year, father heard that if you put a aspirin in the water, the tree would last longer. It did – it lasted for seven days instead of five.

I don't recall ever thinking we needed or desired any more than one present and a sock full of nuts, an orange, and a box of Life Savers. I did dread getting underpants and a tie in the stocking - that seemed to be a waste of good space that could have been filled with hard rock candy. The one present was never an item we asked for. Father didn't believe in writing Santa Claus so a present list was out. Gifts worthy of giving should be items needed, not wanted. This was, of course, a lesson in economics to be used later on in life when you could possibly err in your life "choices." One should always screen ones purchases with a review of "do I need this, or do I want this?"

As I recall, the hard part of Christmas was to explain to all my peers at church why I didn't get two dozen gifts. I found it easy to beat them to the punch by bragging on the one gift that I got to the point that any other gifts would have been a complete waste.

As an adult, married with children, I was now faced with guilt and Christian ethic issues about Christmas present activity that involved what I thought was needless spending and excessive involvement with the Christmas Devil of days gone by. Any force that would get you to spend money you didn't have and pay for it later had to be sin; simple.

I too found myself in Pastor Peterson's shoes; "I daily face the seductions of culture – religion."

Just today in review of the Christmas story in Matthew I rediscovered the giving of gifts by the three Wise Men. All the gifts had great value but a greater revelation came as I realized that it was Baby Jesus who gave those gifts forward to his parents so that they could be blessed. You see, Joseph and Mary had to have funds to live on when they escaped to avoid King Herod. Without those first three gifts, they would have failed and worse, the baby Jesus would have been at risk of death.

Now I've connected a part of my Christmas celebration that brings both the Bible's God Story and my God Story together; may my presents on earth be as in heaven; a blessing to someone else.

Lesson Five ~ I needed a Shekinah story

Pastor Duane & Sue Sheriff have a daughter named Shekinah. For the life of me, I never knew what that name meant or why they would choose such an unusual name for one of their children. If the truth be known, I'd never heard the word, not as an adjective or a noun.

As I continued to read Peterson's book, The Pastor, I was about to get a lesson in Shekinah. Additionally, I did my due diligence and sought other resources to understand the Shekinah. What I found was this: It's an old rabbinic story in Hebrew that refers to a collective vision that brings together dispersed fragments of divinity. Additionally, there is this notion that Shekinah is a disseminating presence that alerts us to the awareness of God at a certain time and in a certain place where you'd never expect God to be.

I never found any reference to Shekinah in the Bible; at least e-sword didn't surface one. The rabbinic story says that it's a selective showing at God's discretion to affirm and encourage or bring a revelation of something that we as individuals don't have eyes to see or understand. So that accounts for the mystical Judaism of the Middle Ages that placed great importance on the Shekinah.

Peterson talks about the Jews returning from their Babylonian captivity. Babylon had been destroyed by Jerusalem and their precious Solomon temple as well. So the Persian king, Cyrus gave the Jews permission to return to their homeland and rebuild.

Peterson says, "Here's what you need to tell Karen and your congregation;" and I quote: "When the first people arrived they took one look at the restored temple and wept at what they saw. As they wept, a dazzling, light-resplendent presence descended, the Shekinah; God's personal presence; and filled that humble, modest, makeshift, sorry excuse for a temple with glory. They were thrilled and lifted their arms high in praise for now the Jews understood being home again. God was truly present.

The Shekinah faded out. The Glory stayed."

In 2010 I had my first go round of major man sickness; I was hospitalized four times in a row at Wilson and Jones and only by the mercy and grace of God am I here today to write about it. I was in room 257.

Right after that hospital run, I started writing a new book named "Church in Room 257." In the end, that book got punched in the computer manuscript with my finger over the "delete" button. The problem was simple – I decided that book needed to be written; not Father God. Shame on me for pushing ahead of His purpose and plans for my life. To say the least, it will get your attention when you fully understand that God has no reason to bless your mess.

The key to my learning curve here was: "What we do in getting ourselves going doesn't look anything like what we expect it to." For Paul in Peterson's book, his congregation worshipped in a three car-garage that didn't look at all like a synagogue. For me, I held church in Room 257 for weeks on end and never understood what it was. There were no choirs singing, there were no children's churches or youth programs, there were no regular service schedules, nobody passed the buckets to take up the offering and the sermon often was adapted to fit the individual that Father God sent to me in the room. Sometimes we had only one in the room; at other times we had up to fifteen in the room. I prayed, I discipled, I quoted and read scriptures, I prayed for healing in other folks and I comforted many in distress. I was so out of touch with was the "real truth," and what was occurring in the room I had to have Pastor Jeff and Pastor Terry tell me that Father God had plunged me into ministry right there right now and without warning. I had visits from God and the Holy Spirit (without the drugs being involved in my recovery) and I had visions. I wrote down everything I heard from Father God and the Holy Spirit on yellow tablets which amounted to six by the time I left the church; I mean the hospital.

Today I understand that I had a Shekinah experience and that's my God Story. Today I understand that the trappings of a church are not a church ~ it was the Body of Christ that was the church and I got to be their pastor. I truly believe this was the beginning of the Care Pastor role that Rhonda and I embarked on.

Lesson Six ~ I'm not your mental health project

God grant me the grace to describe this learning curve without falling off the cliff and returning to "mad." Somewhere between a four year span and my receiving two degrees in Social Work and Sociology, all the pastors I knew were converting themselves and their church settings into para-normal counseling centers.

Someone noticed we didn't have enough therapists and mental health support in the good old USA, so why not embrace the church and their pastors as your backup system? Pastors everywhere were giving up and abandoning their vocation to take up counseling. They sought insight into emotional, mental, and relational difficulties that destroyed people's lives. They declared without much forethought that they, based on being a pastor, were fully able to fix people with problems.

When I was having a personal struggle, I needed spiritual counseling – not a dose of what I was doing Monday through Friday; who needs two Gestalt Therapists gaining access to their mind? Granted, my work in therapy, both individual and group, was bearing fruit in the sense that individuals became aware of their "mess," and therefore had the option to make new choices. There; a complex therapy model in less than 22 words; explained.

When I approached the pastor's study, he was firing questions that sounded more like my intake process than spiritual guidance. The minute he would discover that I had been married and divorced more than once, he would auto shoot his new list of labels at me along with their standard "fixes."

The results were as you would expect. One, I quit going to pastors to find spiritual counseling. Two, I avoided pastors who looked at me like I was one of their prized clients from the pile of congregational inadequacies.

Again, I left, seeking the perfect church.

Eugene Peterson's experiences turned this page of my history into a current understanding of what exactly happened to pastors in the 1970's and 1980's. He said, "The people who made up my congregation had plenty of problems and more than enough inadequacies, but congregation is not defined by its collective problems. Congregation is a company of people who are defined by their creation in the image of God, living souls, whether they know it or not. They are not problems to be fixed, but mysteries to be honored and revered. Who else in the community other than the pastor has the assigned task of greeting men and women and welcoming them into a congregation in which they are known not by what is wrong with them, but who they are, just as they are?"

When I came to Victory Life and found myself seeking spiritual help, I found Care Groups, and I found pastors willing to mentor me in spiritual issues. I found the Word, the Truth, and the activity of walking out your salvation in your daily kingdom walk to be on top of the list. I didn't find another counselor, or Social Worker and certainly no psychiatrists and wanna-bes.

I notice now that the culture has introduced the "required counseling license," with all its trappings to avoid the pitfalls of past counselors. This places me on alert to not get involved with pastors who are being pushed into the cultures notion of what, when, and why they counsel.

Pastor Peterson said, "When people want help with their parents or children or emotions, they do not ordinarily see themselves as wanting help with God. But if I am going to stay true to my vocation as a pastor, I can't let the "market" determine what I do."

Peterson's right; I don't need to fall back on my work as a clinical Social Worker. It's not my job to be the behavior cop. As a Care Pastor, or any other role in serving Christ my job is to find ways to pray with and for people and teach them to pray.

Popeye Harnish

Lesson Seven ~ Heuristic Writing

In a Mennonite school, each grade is a row. Left to right, facing the pupils, you would have 1st grade on row one up to 8th grade on row eight, when you finished row eight school was over. All Mennonite kids return to the farm at the end of the eighth grade. By then, you should be able to read, write, and do math. I never made it all the way through Mennonite schools; instead, I was thrust into English school because father had left the Mennonite faith and went off to Bible Training College in Binghamton, New York. I did however, attend a school so small that the row to row grade system worked.

I remember two things about my early education; namely, I loved to read and write. But two plus two didn't always mean four. Math was insane and full of puzzles never to be known to me. All I wanted out of Math class was the ability to count money. You need money and you need Math to make sure you get what's entitled to you. I did learn to count change and do it correctly.

Some days, I have to laugh in my present years; gave the boy at the window of the ice cream store two dollars and six cents. My bill was $1.36 and my change should have been .70 cents. He had to get a manager.

As the years rushed forward, my opportunity to excel in reading and writing came first in high school. I could read really well and I took excellent notes during the teacher's classroom lecture. My additive feature was to make my own personal notes in the margins just in case the teacher asked us a question during the next lecture. Sure enough, that occurred more than once and my "side writings," allowed me to catch the teacher's eye and end up with a good grade. What a neat trade off; a little effort, a little writing, and a little reading; can't beat that.

As I entered my senior year in high school, my counselor realized I somehow was missing one credit needed to graduate. My options: take the typing class with a room full of girls. Truthfully, I was about to enter into seventh heaven. I could play the piano, so no doubt this typewriter deal could be mastered.

I did graduate with just enough credits and yes I could type 65 words a minute when I left that class; still can fifty-one years later.

Home from the service and off to college at nights. I worked first as a parts chaser for Ingersoll Rand, but later got promoted to sub-assembly foreman over 100 lb ESH machines. Writing reports became second nature. Writing letters of suggestion also became second nature. When I was offered the foreman job, it was noted by the interviewer that my written suggestions showed my interest in Ingersoll Rand as a career, not just a job. Bingo; writing opens the door again.

After Corning College and my first job as a Therapist II for the New York State Department of Mental Health, writing progress notes became a way of life. It was a story, a current review of what was going on in that client's life at that time, in that treatment, and in that long range plan for wellness.

At the University of Texas Arlington, I really started to hone my writing skills. As a Sociologist and Social Work double major to get two degrees, I had to write, write, and do some more writing. My research was going very well as I approached my graduate work and one of the professors asked me to join him and co-author one of his books. I think you can guess who did the drafts, who did the research, and who wrote a large part of the authored works; not the professor. However, the professor was my mentor in writing.

His constant corrections put form into place. It put empirical data into place instead of subjective opinionating. It got me to create my style of writing.

As the years rolled on, writing became a way to make money. Grants, loans, business plans all required a knack for writing. I once heard am old professor say that anyone can do anything as long as they learn the language. Each venture in life requires usage of that enterprises' particular language. Everything has a name, a word associated with its action or reaction. All directives and implementations require words and phrases that signal certain responses.

Then on the Monday that followed my baptism in the Holy
Spirit, I read in the Message Bible two verses from Habakkuk;
para-phrase "What's God going to say to my questions? I'm
braced for the worst. I'll climb to the lookout tower and scan
the horizon. I'll wait to see what God says, how he'll answer
my complaint." Immediately I got my answer in verse two;
"write this, write what you see. Write it out in big block letters
so that it can be read on the run."

From that day on, I wrote my experiences. I quickly learned
that the Bible tells us to share our God Stories with our children
and their children. At first, there was no book in sight. In the
beginning, it started out as a "blog;" a daily "blog" that shared
what God was doing in my life day by day. Later on, the
collection of daily writings became my first published book
Escape From the Southern Comfort Society.

The hills and valleys that my fingers crossed during my writing
for the next season kept bringing new growth to my kingdom
walk. I learned that the high risk of sharing myself, my
thoughts, and my projections took on new meaning. I was
writing what I saw, what I heard, what I read, and what was
internalized as now part of my working out my salvation.

At times, that didn't work to well for me. It certainly didn't win
friends and relatives and it certainly didn't get me on the New
York Times Best Seller's list. Again I found myself turning to
heuristic writing; writing to explore and discover what I didn't
know. At some level, that wasn't working well because I really

didn't understand the dynamics that came with my projections. I still felt disjointed. The Bible was one language and my world was another language. Aside from one hour a week when the pastor would preach, the two worlds didn't meet very often.

Then came another Eugene H. Peterson experience when he talks about the sacred qualities of language. His work as a pastor was immersed in language. My work as a Care Pastor and author was immersed in language.

Peterson went on to say, and I quote from page 239 ~ "My work as a pastor was immersed in language." There was hardly anything I did that did not involve language: the Word of God provided not information but revelation. Jesus told stories and taught and prayed, not to entertain us or inspire us, but to draw us into a participating, believing, listening, loving way of life that was, above all, local and personal; prayerful. I wanted to do that, too. A way of using language in which God, whether implicitly or explicitly, had the first word. And I began to understand that the way I used language involved not just speaking it and writing it, but listening to it ~ listening to the words written in Scripture, but also listening to the words spoken to me by the people in my groups.

This became my bench mark for connection. The Bible God Stories had to connect with the People God Stories to bring about what Peterson calls; "the lived quality of the gospel in their lives." Now I could write forward to the goal of keeping language in motion as the written Word, a biblical word of revelation. This would stop the God talk about the revelation.

In the end, Peterson remarks, "All language, all true language, is not so much communication, getting something said accurately and persuasively, adding to the information and knowledge that can be put in a library. True language has to do with communion, establishing a relationship that makes for life: love and faith and hope, forgiveness and salvation and justice. True language requires both a tongue and an ear."

In my final effort to become a Christian author, I learned from Eugene H. Peterson that god talk ~ depersonalized, non-relational, un-listening language ~ kills. May Father God grant me the wisdom to not engage in god talk.

Chapter 8
Nailing fence boards

This is a God Story about hands. There was a grandfather who started to develop problems with his hands in his late sixties. A trip to town to consult his long-time doctor friend resulted in grandfather learning that his hands and fingers had received so much pressure and abuse over the years farming that he had the onset of arthritis. Although this was the early stages of arthritis, the grandfather didn't get upset and he didn't start having a pity party. In fact, he didn't seem to be mad about it or even come close to throwing a fit.

At the time, his grandson, Pete Junior, was spending the summer with grandfather and grandmother to not only help out, but to escape the hot concrete in the city. This summer's long visit had become a standard tradition that pleased the grandparents big time. Certainly Pete Junior's mom, grandfather's daughter, didn't mind the relief of having to take care of one less child over the summer time.

Pete Junior just seemed to fit the bill. He was way more interested in farming than working at a gas station, washing cars, or mowing lawns in the city for money. This particular year Pete Junior had just turned sixteen years of age. Big, strong, good looking, and starting to make a hand, Pete Junior seemed made for the farm. In fact, grandfather told Pete Junior he had earned the right to be a paid farm hand this year and his starting wages would be ten dollars a day for a day's work. For Pete Junior, that added up to money to buy a truck. At ten dollars a day, six days a week at sixty dollars, and $240.00 a month for three months – why, that added up to $720.00. All he had to do then was earn the other $280.00 and he could buy Mr. Brownlee's old Chevy half ton truck. Visions of driving to high school in his own truck certainly danced in his head that night.

As the summer began, grandfather gave Pete Junior more responsible jobs. Today he was to drag the field – but when grandfather got over there, Pete Junior was on his knees beside the tractor just cussing up a storm. Pete Junior had forgot to check the oil and gas in the tractor that morning and here it was – out of gas and dead in the water. As his anger mounted up inside, Pete Junior threw the tractor's gas cap across the field as far as it could go. Grandfather never said a word. He walked across most of the field and spotted where the gas cap had landed, picked it up and strolled back across the field towards his truck. "Get in PJ, we need to go get gas," he said.

As time passed, grandfather noticed that the charming sixteen year old grandson had a temper that often got discharged without any thought at all. The need to always be in a rush kept the lad fairly well tangled up most every day of the week.

Back at the house that evening, grandfather asked PJ to go to the shop and fetch up the bucket of odd nails and a framing 22 oz. hammer. When PJ returned with hammer and bucket in hand, grandfather motioned him up behind the tool shed to the wooden fence. "PJ, I know you have been having trouble with your temper. I'd like to help you overcome that trait and see if what you're getting mad over is really worth all that fussing and that cussing you're doing." PJ hung his head in shame. It never was PJ's intent to upset his grandfather.

Grandfather said, "How many times did you get mad today?' PJ thought for a minute and realized he had thrown a hissy fit at least four times. "Son, go pound four of those 10 penny nails into that fence in a straight line." PJ did exactly as he was told. "Now," grandfather said, "every night after supper, you pound in a nail for every time you get upset and cuss. Do you understand?" PJ nodded his head.

At the end of summer, PJ came to grandfather and said, "Look – the bucket is empty." "Good,' grandfather said, "Now every day you don't get mad or upset and cuss, go pull one of those nails out." Again, PJ was proud that he had control over his temper and day after day, more nails were returned to that old rusty bucket.

The last day of the summer, PJ pointed out to grandfather that all the nails were back in the bucket and it had been weeks since his last blow up.

Grandfather acknowledged the lad's victory over his temper and he inquired, "How did you change that habit of blowing up?" PJ sort of bowed his head and explained that he knew he could not stop getting mad so he had prayed to Father God for help. "Every time I had to drive that nail in the fence, I realized what price Jesus paid for my sins on the cross and how much those nails had to hurt. Honestly, grandfather, I was ashamed and I asked for forgiveness too."

"Good," grandfather said, "But son, there's one more lesson to be learned over getting mad and going off like a Roman candle. Look at that fence now. Do you see all the holes that are left behind? "Yes sir, I do." "That's the problem with blowing up – you can never take back what comes out after the fact. The Bible says we should guard our heart and watch our words, for they can destroy. I think you've learned this lesson well. Take that learning with you, grandson, for the rest of your life – and you'll never regret what you say."

As PJ loaded up in his father's truck to return to the city, he noticed the leather looking worn out hands of his grandfather. There was a man who had drove a lot of nails in his life straight as ever; very few ever had to be pulled out; just like his words. Thank you Father God for my grandfather and the lessons on the fence.

Chapter 9
Your grandparent's closet

The one thing we always expect from our grandparents is love, kindness, forgiveness, and support. Ninety nine percent of us have great memories and God Stories of grandparents that have passed on and ninety nine percent of us who still have grandparents living will instantly tell you they love seeing and spending time with memaw and pepaw. However, in a fallen world, the last place we look for "bones in the closet," is at Memaw's and Pepaw's house. There is an old saying that says, "If you look in anyone's closet, there are old bones in there that don't need to be uncovered." That phrase refers to people not being perfect. In fact, it typifies exactly what the Bible says in Romans.

Romans 3:23 "For all have sinned, and come short of the glory of God." It's very clear that none of us can escape sin. It's also noteworthy that all of us "come short" of the glory of God. Try as we may, we will fail at times.

This chapter exposes the "bones from your grandparent's closet;" their past, if you will. The perfect, or near perfect, grandparents that you have come to know is now a product of years of grace and forgiveness from Father God. It's a sign of maturity in the faith that they maintain their walk on the narrow road. Their awareness is very different from yours; they see a larger, bigger picture called life – whereas you probably still focus on you and what's up tomorrow.

For starters, the grandparents that shared these short God Stories have done so in hopes that you will see the light before the darkness overtakes you in life. It's not about being perfect – it's about being forgiven and being renewed in the body, soul, and spirit.

It's a "can" statement: "You can avoid this pitfall, this sin; it's your choice."

Child Protective Services said ~ "In September, 2008, in Tucson, AZ two grandparents were arrested for child abuse."

I quote a post from Miss Pearl on September 8, 2008; "Tucson, AZ - A 9-year-old boy, whose name is being withheld, was found last Saturday locked in a bedroom closet surrounded by feces and urine. He was severely malnourished, weighing only 48 pounds and looked "pale" according to the arresting deputy. The clinic worker knew something was wrong immediately because besides his shocking appearance, the 9-year-old could not read or write. Turns out he's never been enrolled in school.

Instead, he's been living out his days in a closet measuring 49" x 41", sleeping on a urine and feces soaked sleeping bag – and from the description of his condition, doing nothing else.

The grandparents have been raising the child, along with his 8-year-old brother since birth. Becky said their mother dropped them off and they haven't heard from her in years. Thankfully, it appears the 8-year-old was spared the abuse and has been attending public school. Both children are now in CPS custody.

None of us can begin to understand grandparents that would do such evil to a child. However, if the shock of this horrid event overtakes your sense of fairness and reality, remember to always remain alert to changes. What we see is not always what we get. Nobody likes to expose or be involved in such life-changing events – but to make it a better world, someone always has to be willing to be involved.

Remember – the Bible always holds our answers and our truth.

Matthew 18:6 "But whoso shall offend one of these little ones which believe in me, it were better for him that a millstone were hanged about his neck, and *that* he were drowned in the depth of the sea."

Matthew 18:10 "Take heed that ye despise not one of these little ones; for I say unto you,

That in heaven their angels do always behold the face of my Father which is in heaven."

Matthew 18:14 "Even so it is not the will of your Father which is in heaven, that one of

these little ones should perish."

Section 2
Behind This Entrance is all the "one liners."

Chapter 10
Things your grandparents wanted to tell you ~

One Liner One

 PawPaw spent his entire life on a ranch. He was born on a ranch, raised on a ranch, and lived on a ranch his entire life. In the end, Pawpaw died on his ranch far off in the south pasture with only a herd of mother cows as his last witness.

The better part of PawPaw's life was spent going to the same small community church that stood the test of time for nearly one hundred and fifty years. In his youth, they had several full time pastors; but as the years rolled on, the sixty or so ranchers and their families could not afford a pastor's salary and all the expenses. Soon the church only had a monthly pastor who traveled the circuit to bring the good news to several smaller churches. PawPaw always knew the Sunday of the month that the circuit pastor would preach. That Sunday we knew exactly where PawPaw wanted us: in church.

As time passed, I noticed PawPaw seemed to withdraw and I'd catch him reading his Bible, but also another book. When I got a chance to see, I noticed it was a book of poems. Poems, mind you. At first, I thought it very strange for PawPaw to read poems.

As you would expect, very little gets by most grandfathers and so it was when I got caught peeking in the poem book. That moment when you know beyond any doubt that you have been caught red handed, you have only one defense. Sorry.

As PawPaw reached out his old leather worn hand and placed it on my shoulder, he thumbed through the book of poems and said, "If nothing else I ever tell you makes any sense, you can believe this poem. With Christmas just around the corner this will make all your future Christmas celebrations have meaning. Go ahead now, and read this poem to me out loud."

I picked up the book and started; "This is a poem by S. Omar Barker."

A Cowboy's Christmas Prayer

I ain't much good at prayin',

and You may not know me, Lord --

For I ain't much seen in churches,

where they preach Thy Holy Word.

But you may have observed me

out here on the lonely plains,

A-lookin' after cattle,

feelin' thankful when it rains.

Admirin' Thy great handiwork.

the miracle of the grass,

Aware of Thy kind Spirit,

in the way it comes to pass

That hired men on horseback

and the livestock that we tend

Can look up at the stars at night,

and know we've got a Friend.

So here's ol' Christmas comin' on,

remindin' us again

Of Him whose coming brought good will

into the hearts of men.

A cowboy ain't a preacher, Lord,

but if You'll hear my prayer,

I'll ask as good as we have got

for all men everywhere.

Don't let no hearts be bitter, Lord.

Don't let no child be cold.

Make easy the beds for them that's sick

and them that's weak and old.

Let kindness bless the trail we ride,

no matter what we're after,

And sorter keep us on Your side,

in tears as well as laughter.

I've seen ol' cows a-starvin' -

and it ain't no happy sight;

Please don't leave no one hungry, Lord,

on Thy Good Christmas Night --

No man, no child, no woman,

and no critter on four feet

I'll do my doggone best

to help you find 'em chuck to eat.

I'm just a sinful cowpoke, Lord --

ain't got no business prayin'

But still I hope you'll ketch a word

or two, of what I'm sayin':

We speak of Merry Christmas, Lord--

I reckon You'll agree --

There ain't no Merry Christmas
for nobody that ain't free!

So one thing more I ask You,
Lord: just help us what You can
To save some seeds of freedom
for the future Sons of Man!

S. Omar Barker;

In December, 2013 the S. Omar Barker estate let us know that this poem is now considered in the public domain.

One Liner Two

Grandmother needs you to know "There's more to life."

I think the most important thing I would want my grandchildren (who are all teenagers or older) to know is: There's more to life than education, jobs, video games, clothes and material gain. All of these "things" are what we "do" in life, but they aren't the most important thing in life. It is about what Jesus did for us on the Cross. Our Father God had the plan of redemption. (We all fall short of the glory of God.) Jesus carried out the plan, and the Holy Spirit is here on the earth with us to comfort us, teach us and lead us into all the truth. It is not about man-made religion of do's and don'ts, or religious edifices… called churches. It is about fellow believers being the church. It's about loving each other and making memories. We are supposed to share our testimonies and encourage one another. That's why we share our God Stories.

When we say, "It's not about you, hot rod; it is about Him," we mean things like: Life isn't fair. Our battle is not against flesh and blood as Christians. There is a god (little g) of this world

(Satan), but as Christians, we have the greater One (Jesus) Who has overcome him. We are in a battle, and he is trying to steal the Word of God that dwells in us. Don't let him. It's not about you, hot rod, it is about HIM. It's about the Kingdom of Heaven on earth, and until Jesus comes again, we are in a battle. Jesus in us IS the hope of glory; we have overcome through HIM. Mat 5:5 "You're blessed when you're content with just who you are--no more, no less. That's the moment you find yourselves proud owners of everything that can't be bought."

One Liner Three

Grandmother Jerry Hunsinger wants you to know that "It's important that you teach your children to love Jesus."

In my first book, *Escape from the Southern Comfort Christian Society*, you will find a chapter that contains the miracle of walking the love of Jesus out in your daily kingdom walk. The main two characters are the team of Grandmother Jerry Hunsinger and my bride, Grandmother Rhonda L Harnish. Their ministry was the "basket ministry" that I coined the VL Hunt Club. Grandmother Jerry had been the mainstay of this ministry, including finding baskets and hundreds of usable items to decorate each gift basket. New folks who arrived at Victory Life Sherman were treated to a back-up call along with a welcome basket. This seemingly normal everyday church event was anything but normal; it was "but God." I urge you to read the VL Hunt Club God Story; it will warm your heart.

Her children and grandchildren will always be blessed with her advice.

One Liner Four

A grandmother wanted me to pass this on so her grandkids got the opportunity to see this some day.

A Minister passing through his church

In the middle of the day,

Decided to pause by the altar

To see who came to pray.

Just then the back door opened,

And a man came down the aisle,

The minister frowned as he saw the man

Hadn't shaved in a while.

His shirt was torn and shabby,

And his coat was worn and frayed,

The man knelt down and bowed his head,

Then rose and walked away.

In the days that followed at precisely noon,

The preacher saw this chap,

Each time he knelt just for a moment,

A lunch pail in his lap.

Well, the minister's suspicions grew,

With robbery a main fear,

He decided to stop and ask the man,

'What are you doing here?'

The old man said he was a factory worker

And lunch was half an hour

Lunchtime was his prayer time,

For finding strength and power.

I stay only a moment

Because the factory's far away;

As I kneel here talking to the Lord,

This is kinda what I say:

'I just came by to tell You, Lord,

How happy I have been,

Since we found each other's friendship

And You took away my sin.

Don't know much of how to pray,

But I think about You every day.

So, Jesus, this Is Ben,

Just checking in today.'

The minister feeling foolish,

Told Ben that it was fine.

He told the man that he was welcome

To pray there anytime.

'It's time to go, and thanks,' Ben said

As he hurried to the door.

Then the minister knelt there at the altar,

Which he'd never done before.

His cold heart melted, warmed with love,

As he met with Jesus there.

As the tears flowed down his cheeks,

He repeated old Ben's prayer:

'I just came by to tell You, Lord,

How happy I have been,

Since we found each other's friendship

And You took away my sin.

Don't know much of how to pray,

But I think about You every day.

So, Jesus, this Is me,

Just checking in today.'

Past noon one day, the minister noticed

That old Ben hadn't come.

As more days passed and still no Ben,

He began to worry some.

At the factory, he asked about him,

Learning he was ill.

The hospital staff was worried,

But he'd given them a thrill.

The week that Ben was with them,

Brought changes in the ward.

His smiles and joy contagious.

Changed people were his reward.

The head nurse couldn't understand

Why Ben could be so glad,

When no flowers, calls or cards came,

Not a visitor he had.

The minister stayed by his bed,

He voiced the nurse's concern:

No friends had come to show they cared.

He had nowhere to turn.

Looking surprised, old Ben spoke up

And with a winsome smile;

'The nurse is wrong, she couldn't know,

He's been here all the while.'

Every day at noon He comes here,

A dear friend of mine, you see,

He sits right down and takes my hand,

Leans over and says to me:

'I just came by to tell you, Ben,

How happy I have been,

Since we found this friendship,

And I took away your sin.

I think about you always

And I love to hear you pray,

And so Ben, this is Jesus,

Just checking in today.'

If this blesses you, pass it on. Many people will walk in and out of your life, but only

true friends will leave footprints in your heart...

May God hold you in the palm of His hand

And Angels watch over you..

Please pass this on to your friends & loved ones.

So, FRIENDS & FAMILY, this is ME ...

"Just Checking In Today"

Section 3
The Harnish Garden

Popeye Harnish

Chapter 11
Popeye's Round Pen Salvation

Oh my, this has got my attention. I've arrived at what could be the most important choice of words that have ever been written by me. This ride is my last ditch effort to impart wisdom and knowledge to my children and my grandchildren. As excited as I am to have this opportunity, I find myself shaking in my boots like it was my first ride out of the chute. My fingers are gripping the keys with the notion that a steady hand will at least give me a chance to ride the full 8 seconds. I reach up and pull my hat down and nod at the gate keeper and yell, "Let'r rip."

I can't begin to tell you how much time I've spent trying to fully understand what it was I needed you to know. I struggled with the format, I struggled with the words, and I struggled with the subject matter. I prayed about it, I outlined it, and right up to the time I climbed over the wall and onto this bucking bull, I wasn't sure I could do the full 8 seconds. What I quickly grasped was I somehow had slipped into the ditch of "self," just long enough to think I was doing this by myself.

Now the Holy Spirit has jerked me back just long enough to realize that the entire Trinity – Father, Son, and Holy Spirit were all part of this. So you should not be surprised that I am ready and willing to give it "our," all.

In my world, I'm concerned that all the "Church talk," all the "Sunday School talk,' all The "Youth for Christ talk," all your summer camps, and even your time spent reading the Bible has left you with a zillion questions that are unanswered. I'm afraid you have faked it till you make it because you wanted to please your parents, your peers, your teachers, and your pastor, and me and Saint Rhonda. I sense you are just dying to get away on your own so you don't have to go to church.

Some of you have already made it past the magical number eighteen and have left home for college. How's that working for you? Some have returned to the mother land and seem to be seeking your place in life. Some are now married and you even have your own family to start raising.

This is good because all of you will recognize our "garden." Home is home and always will be. God planted each man/family in their own garden. It's our world and we are blessed to have it. Granted, we have differences – different houses, different jobs, and different educations – but in the end, we all are that "one family: the Harnish bunch."

I think the key for me in talking to all of you is to simply tell you some stories from my years here on planet earth. At times I wasn't serving God, I certainly wasn't seeking to be told "well done good and faithful servant." Granted I got saved when I was five years old and my father and mother certainly grew us boys up in a full gospel home and church.

What didn't happen was I didn't become a missionary, or a preacher, or even a director of music at some church. I didn't go to a Christian college, and I didn't stay at one church for a long time. What I did do was attend church when I felt guilty or when I was down and out and needed something from God. I came from the school of Good Boy vs. Bad Boy and fully recognized that I would respond to that model when things were going bad. Once I recovered from whatever set back I was having at the time, I'd let God go and walk out of the room again, content that I indeed had something to do with my recovery.

I always saw myself as a self-made man. I had a better work ethic than most, I'd always try and win, regardless of the cost. And I always thought I could move up on the success ladder if I just worked long enough and hard enough. I never collected unemployment and I often worked more than one job at a time to get ahead.

By the age of 59, I had about exhausted all my resources – only to find that I was not happy, did not have enough, and could not figure out what my next move should be. My dreams of that life-long job were gone; hence, no retirement available. My collection of "stuff," wasn't nearly as impressive as I had thought it would be. Certainly, my ability to stay married didn't work out. I was the champion of getting married to someone that needed me to fix their broken wing – but as soon as they were sound enough to travel and fly, they disappeared out of my world. That only ended up counting against me; married too many times.

I also failed as a father. I missed initial contact with my girl and two boys at an early age; and instead of coming back and being the father I should have been, I kept traveling west and avoided parenting responsibilities altogether. The only thing I did right was pay child support every time and on time. Finally, I married Saint Rhonda twenty-five years ago and I attempted to "be the father" to the four children she brought to the marriage in the package deal. Back then, I was sure I could handle being the new "instant mashed potato daddy," and quickly found out my favorite trait with the kids was being "1st National Bank Daddy."

So life charged on at full bore and I was driven to be something I didn't even acknowledge or understand. I tried to be someone else; never just me.

Five years ago, after two failed church attendance attempts, I ended up going to Victory Life Church on Texoma Parkway in the old McCoy's lumber yard building. After the first message I head Pastor Duane Sheriff preach, we never missed a church service unless it was snow, ice, or sickness.

This was the beginning of my new life in Christ and I declare it was the day my old self was packed up and put away in the closet. Not "some things" changed; everything changed. I never felt so hungry for God and the Word than that after initial event. Finally! I'm sitting under someone with enough nerve to preach the truth and back it up with chapter and verse.

I can't begin to tell you what your life will be like the day you give yourself totally over to the Lord. You will just have to live it out yourself.

So, let's ride on down this trail and see what I can bring to the dinner plate. These God

Stories are from the heart and as such I offer them to you – not as answers, but as questions you need to answer for yourself.

Chapter 12

Teo's Story; the mystery cowboy

The dawn had inched its way up over the back hill and across the hay field just in time to burst this high intense beam of sunlight right down the middle aisle covering about four or five box stalls. Two year old Quarter Horse cutting prospects did their snicker, snort, and box stall dance as we pushed the oat cart down to the next feeder. The sweet smell of good coastal hay left the horse barn smelling like heaven. I glanced down to make sure the help was getting their part done and we could get this show on the road.

I had taken two young cowboys under my wing that summer, and I had this mystery Caballero, wetback, cowboy named Teo who showed up out of the clear blue sky sharply at five a.m., come rain or shine and always corrected me saying he was a Vaquero, not a Caballero. I used to love getting under his skin with my lack of Spanish speaking ability. I was mostly hand signals back then, with an occasional Andale, Andale, which meant, "Let's get moving," so most of what he was saying rolled off the end of my ears.

Later on, as I got to know Teo, I took the time to look up the differences in Mexican horse trainers; Teo was right – he did come from a long line of outstanding Vaqueros and yes, they were the best of the best.

Teo was the biggest mystery man I had ever known in my life. I think we hit it off for two reasons; one, Teo didn't talk – he did the program. The truth is this rag-tailed little old bush beater of a Mexican horse trainer had more talent than any trainer I had ever met or worked with. This guy was a jewel hiding in the brush alongside some West Texas highway, with only one thing on his mind: get a horse job somewhere. The second reason we hit it off was Teo was as honest as the day was long.

The first day I saw Teo could have been his last day on earth. I spotted him down by the tack room and I thought he was an early morning thief looking to rip me off. Had something been missing when I got to the tack room, I'd have hunted him down and shot his happy butt.

Teo was a brave man when I confronted him that morning. "Job," he said. I can remember firing back at him with, "I can't afford no wet back and I ain't got no job so go on."

"Me free, Senor Capitan."

Free? What kind of game was this sawed off little shotgun talking about? Free? Of all the gall! He just walked right straight past me to the first box stall on the right. He looked me straight in the eye and quickly took the gray mare to the horse walker, hooked her up and started her round and round. On his way back, he grabbed the wheelbarrow and pitchfork, and started to muck her stall and put in fresh bedding. Later that afternoon I reached in my pants for a cigarette and found a stray five dollar bill in there, so I got it out to pay ole Teo. As I glanced around the barn and outside by the round pen, there was no Teo to be found. He showed up at the barn at 5:30 a.m. the next morning and disappeared at 6 p.m. that evening. He was like the wind - at first, you would not realize he was there – and then when you chased him, he would disappear.

When Friday came around, I handed each of my helpers their cash wages for the week, and off to town we would go for supper. As I approached Teo with five dollar an hour wages he refused, and disappeared again. Now I'm thinking, this guy is not for real; he's free; really free. Of course, I was still on the defensive side with him and I wasn't about to let go and find myself turned upside down with emotions.

The second week arrived, and here comes old Teo down the bunny trail. Again at week's end, we had the informal Friday cash wage routine going on and I pushed two weeks worth of wages towards Teo to pay him.

Next thing I know, one of my students for the summer started to tell me in English what Teo was saying to him in Spanish. The words were not complete and the phrases; well, you figure it out. The idea was Teo only wanted the right to work here because he loved the horses and I didn't beat him up every day.

Beat him up? Are you kidding? I asked the student, What in the hell is he talking about?" They chatted for about three minutes and then the student told me how other trainers and ranchers would work him to the bone and they would start drinking and then start punching on the help. Just because we're wet backs doesn't mean we are not people, he told my guy. Because I'd never raised a hand at him, he thought I was a saint. He also liked me because I didn't drink and I had a Bible in the house. I wondered how he knew that.

I guess that was the straw that broke the camel's back. I took Teo around the end of the bunk house and showed him my camper trailer. I unlocked the door and tossed him a key with one word; Casa. Here's your new home, big boy. Later after supper, I stopped by Wal-Mart and got a bag of beans, some flour, some salt, some sugar, taco meat, taco shells, and a bag of chips. I think there was about a dozen other items of food that Teo probably had never seen in his entire life. Again I took out his cash wages, stuffed them in an old bank bag, and set everything on his front steps. I knocked on the door and walked away.

Little did I know that Teo was peeking through the side curtain of the trailer to see what was getting near his new Casa. This new routine never stopped me keeping his weekly wages at five dollars. The following day, I found the bank bag on the front seat of my dually. All his wages were inside that bag.

Again, I'm thinking this dude is free. He's working to have a place to live; wrong.

If my memory serves me correctly, somewhere around a month, the fourth Friday came about and of course it was cash payday again. This time Teo said, "Post office." Post office it was. As we pulled up to the parking spots, I reached under the seat and handed him his bank bag with every dime I owed him. He smiled like a cat that just ate the family pet bird. In we went and right up to the counter he went and he purchased a money order, and stamps. As he filled his money order out, I realized that he was sending 95% of his wages somewhere back to Mexico.

Teo was with me almost two years and late that second year he came to me just before Christmas and said his mother was very ill back in ole Mexico and could he leave and have his job back when he returned? "Of course," I said, and "what else do you need from me?" "Senor, I have need of nothing." The next morning I took Teo to the bus stop with a ticket I purchased for him to El Paso and I slapped a couple of hundred dollar bills into his hand shake. I tipped my hat to him and walked away to the truck. By mile two on my way back to the barn, I realized I was already missing my new best friend.

That friendship occurred back in 1983 in Gainesville, Texas. I was training horses for a big time contractor and Doctor Stormer's dad out of Muenster, Texas. I had seven or eight Delta Airline Captains with prospects in my barn and I was finally a Texas cowboy earning a living as a horse trainer.

At the time, I attended a local Baptist church when I went to church; but living for the Lord was not evident by any fruit for sure. I'd go just enough to get just enough feel good messages so I would not have to go again for a few months. Today, some thirty one years later my time spent with Teo has transformed itself into a God Story I never expected to learn about.

Teo was indeed a part of my story. The greater lesson of Teo was born out of a pure love for both animals and people. Teo was a connected God Story on earth to some God Stories that I read in the Bible.

Notice some of Teo's characteristics: One, he appears out of nowhere, Two, he didn't talk about how great he was; he just did the program, Three, he was honest and didn't have hidden agendas, Four, Teo was brave and stood his ground over one word, job. Five, Teo had a compassionate heart for others and only Teo would have ever thought to offer himself as "free; without wages" to gain access to his heaven on earth.

So the question is: Who in the Bible appears out of nowhere to help you in life? The tie-in God Story to the Teo God Story comes from John, chapter 14, verse 16 and I quote: "I will talk to the Father, and he'll provide you another Friend so that you will always

So the question is: Who in the Bible doesn't talk much; he just does the program; the job at hand? The tie-in God Story to the

Teo God Story comes from the God Story about a day laborer. The Bible says a day laborer needed his pay every day to get food for himself and his family. To withhold the pay for one's gain or convenience created a hardship and was off limits. Deuteronomy 24: 14-15, "Don't abuse a laborer who is destitute and needy, whether he is a fellow Israelite living in your land and in your city."

Deuteronomy 24:15 "Pay him at the end of each workday; he's living from hand to mouth and needs it now. If you hold back his pay, he'll protest to GOD and you'll have sin on your books."

So the question is: Who in the Bible gets beat up just for serving the master? The tie-in Bible God Story is this: The apostles' response would set a precedent for other Christians who would be persecuted. Instead of complaining or feeling sorry for themselves, they rejoiced that they were counted worthy by God to endure the abuse.

So the question is: Who in the Bible took you by the hand and told you "This is your place on earth; now tend to it and keep it." The tie-in Bible God Story was written in Genesis 1: 26-28 paraphrase: "The garden was perfectly prepared. It was man's home and he had to tend and keep it." Even the Biblical paradise required work. (Gen_1:26-28)

So the question is: Who in the Bible would take care of the poor and widows? I Timothy 5:8 - Anyone who neglects to care for family members in need denies the faith. That's worse than refusing to believe in the first place.

Do you see that five different God Stories out of the Bible that became my earthboundreality discovery of my friend Teo? What the Bible God Story shows is exactly what life shows day after day.

It starts to make sense, then, that our relationship with God is born out of our daily lives here on earth. God is not limited to words that come from Sunday services. I learned a couple of other points from Eugene H. Peterson this past year; they are (paraphrased from his book Christ Plays In Ten Thousand Places ~) " It happens; we do not make it happen. The more we get involved in what God is doing, the less we find ourselves running things; the more we participate in God's work as revealed in Jesus, the more is done to us and the more is done through us."

"The more we practice resurrection, the less we are on our own or by ourselves, for we find that this resurrection that is so intensely and relationally personal in Father, Son, and Spirit at the same time, plunges us into relationships with brothers and sisters we never knew we had; we are in community whether we like it or not."

"We do not choose to be in this community; by virtue of the resurrection of Jesus, this is the company we keep."

If every other word I write to you children falls on deaf ears, I hope you see that "life," is more about your Teo experiences.

It's the little unnoticed Teo prints that are so available when you glance in your rear view mirror. It's the Teo prints that enable you to go forward and serve God with full understanding that it's a FROG deal (Fully Rely On God).

Popeye Harnish

Chapter 13
Living In Two Worlds

I'm very concerned that each of you see my focus on "words." Perhaps it's just a by-product of being a writer or it merits everything I think it does. We live in a world of two word sets. We have the Bible "word sets," and we have the world's "word sets." The goal is always to bring those two sets together in harmony with God's plan for our lives.

This notion of the clashing two word sets simply came from years of hearing King James Bible teachings with all their KJV words that I didn't understand and then hearing what the church had to say and not clearly getting all of that language. I remember all too well the phrase: "rightly divide the Word." As a ten year old or perhaps even as old as a new teenager, I thought that rightly divide the word directive could only be for the elders or the pastor. Who did I know that could rightly divide much of anything? Every time I asked a Bible question, I got the runaround or, "Some day, you'll understand." Sunday School teachers, and even pastors often dodged the questions because, truthfully, they didn't get it, either. So they sure were not going to place themselves in the light of being "less than." So they jumped around the Word, or worse yet, they put their own spin on it and made the Word adapt to their needs on earth as it never could have been in heaven.

This discovery of a two world set of words also shines light on why many young adults walk away from church in their early twenties. Granted, new outside influences - like going away to college - can do it; but deep down inside, it's a measure of really not understanding all the phrases and buzz words. When a person is thrust into the educational circle, they are getting fed so much new information that "real truth" becomes almost an obsession. The studies they are undertaking have nothing to do with which truth; it's just that truth is raining everywhere they turn. The problem is they are not turning and walking back into the same church they grew up in. For a season, they decide that old church can just entertain grandma and grandpaw.

Now my focus with you will turn to some new truths that I have received long past my life span of being in whatever story I was in at the time. Because I've always been involved in farming or ranching; mostly horses, I'm going to use the simple words of being just that: a farmer, a rancher, and a horse trainer.

Chapter 14
Truths From The Round Pen

I can remember thinking that whatever was going on with the horse I had in the round pen there was this tie back to what I saw Jesus doing. In my mind, the idea of training young horses was no different than being a pastor of a small church. If, in fact, I could tie the Bible God Stories to the Everyday God Stories in our garden, we would become "more better," at allowing God to work in our lives.

See if this brings about any new understanding for your life.

I saw this in the Bible: The world doesn't fight fair.

I saw this in the pen: The horse could care less if he decides to fight you

2 Cor. 10:3 "The world is unprincipled. It's dog-eat-dog out there! The world doesn't fight fair. But we don't live or fight our battles that way--never have and never will."

How many times have I stepped into that round pen with a brand new prospect: many is a good count. It's so normal to eyeball a colt or filly and size them up with thoughts of how you think they are going to take to training. The surprise is always when the opposite occurs. You will indeed find yourself saying, "Where did that come from?"

I also see such a direct connection between this garden experience and what God teaches us in the Bible. The world is very mean-spirited in many of their ways. Law enforcement often gets a bad rap, but the justice system at large is the monster hidden under the bushes. I've often warned all you kids to avoid the circumstances that get you close to that system; you will not like the results. Enough said.

I saw this in the Bible: God had a plan for us before we were born

I saw this in the pen: Our plan: this horse will be a future cutting horse prospect

<u>Job 25:2</u> "God is sovereign, God is fearsome-- everything in the cosmos fits and works in his plan."

<u>Prov. 16:9</u> "We plan the way we want to live, but only GOD makes us able to live it."

When you look back in your rear view mirror of life, you'll begin to sense that things happen for a reason. It's God. God never leaves us and I believe He stays engaged at every opportunity there is - even when we keep running out of the room and using our "free will." When the Bible says God works in His plan, remember - you have a plan just like I do and everyone else. I pray for each moment in your life when you finally recognize the greatness of God. I pray for the day that you turn your life over to Father God full time and serve him. The rewards of relationship with God cannot be written in words - it's life and you're promised it can be more abundantly.

I saw this in the Bible: God creates; He never stops with you from birth to the grave

I saw this in the pen: We never stop creating the potential of this horse

<u>Eph. 2:10</u> "No, we neither make nor save ourselves. God does both the making and saving. He creates each of us by Christ Jesus to join him in the work he does, the good work he has gotten ready for us to do, work we had better be doing."

Some things in life take on a very firm stance and meaning: The Trinity (God the Father, Jesus the Son, and the Holy Spirit) brings the power of life through non-stop creation. It's a cycle that's never broken in our world and in our lives. Learning to see Jesus, understanding Father God in relationship with you, and seeing the Holy Spirit move in signs, wonders, and miracles in your life can only bring about joy and peace in knowing you will live beyond the grave. Don't ever take God's love for granted.

I saw this in the Bible: God gave us a helper and we formed a relationship

I saw this in the pen: The trainer was given a horse to form a finished relationship

<u>Gen_2:18</u> "GOD said, "It's not good for the Man to be alone; I'll make him a helper, a companion."

After days and weeks in the round pen, the horse you started with changes; be it a colt or filly - they evolve into an understanding of what's expected of them in the relationship with the trainer. Together, they start pushing towards the goal - the finished work of the pen. Then comes the day of glory when you and the colt step into the larger pen and begin to grow to the next level of expertise. Now we add cattle to the puzzle and now we begin to learn how to pick and choose. In the end, we have a cutting horse and a rider who together can control one cow away from the herd. That ability to hold one out goes against all of the natural occurrences in herd work. Herds stick together.

The key is the relationship between horse and rider. That's exactly what occurs in your marriage with your partner. You spend day after day learning how to work together, and in the end, you can handle most everything. The years roll on and you find that your relationship has formed a generational family that says, "As for me and my house, we will serve the Lord." That's a blessed family.

I saw this in the Bible: God gave mankind a place to live called a garden

I saw this in the pen: The rancher built a round pen and said this is for training

Gen. 2:15 "GOD took the Man and set him down in the Garden of Eden to work the ground and keep it in order."

It's totally possible, but very difficult, to train and start a fresh horse outside of a round pen. Granted, lots of methods have been tried from bucking them out to you name it; but nothing has ever worked better than the round pen. It's the pen that holds the key to creation and a finished horse.

When I realized that each of us were also given our own "round pen" by Father God; except He named it "Garden of Eden," the picture ties together without a hitch. We have a designated place on this earth. Our personal Garden of Eden is exactly what you think it is. It's your apartment, your house, your farm, or your ranch. It could be your cabin or even a tent for a season. That space, that area that you inhabit, is exactly where God gives you your foundation.

Just thinking about Gardens gives me some additional understanding. There are always weeds to hoe and we need to keep up with ours. There are always seeds to plant and crops to harvest. God never stops creation, and when we serve Him, we also find that we remain in concert with creation.

I saw this in the Bible: A little sin, like eating apples, can turn into murder

I saw this in the pen: A little fault can end up being a major hole in the horse

Psalm 38:18 "I'm ready to tell my story of failure, I'm no longer smug in my sin."

Well, here's your reality check: everyone sins. Nobody escapes. I was startled at how quickly sin started in the garden and how quickly it led to murder between two brothers. That's a giant leap from the sin of an apple to murder. The Psalms encourage us to confess our sins and our stories of failure. The best part is Father God is faithful and just to forgive us our sins.

As I look out over the walls of the round pen, I realize that a small fault in training a horse can work its way into a giant problem down the road. It can be just a simple thing, like letting the colt get away with being on the wrong lead when you change directions. If you leave that unattended, there will come a day that the horse is behind and can't catch the cow or he'll back off in defeat without trying at all. Worse yet, left untended, your prize cutting horse will start to scotch and cheat you in the corners.

I saw this in the Bible: God gave us all individual names; we are not faceless

I saw this in the pen: Each horse deserves a name to be called by

<u>Josh. 7:14</u> "First thing in the morning you will be called up by tribes. The tribe GOD names will come up clan by clan; the clan GOD names will come up family by family; and the family GOD names will come up man by man."

I can't image not starting my relationship with a horse that was nameless. Of course, the opposite would be to try and call them by their complete name as it shows on their papers. Thank goodness for nicknames. My first horse I ever owned was a Quarter Horse named Silence is Golden. I called him Si. Si was a very personable type horse who stayed engaged with me anytime I was around him. He would nicker when I showed up; perhaps it was more of a nicker to get oats quicker. In the mountains, I could encourage him with the verbal usage of his name and he would respond.

God also made sure that mankind did not end up being a faceless mob. The long list of names and families and tribes in the Bible certainly are proof of Father God's need to have a personal relationship with each person. Have you ever noticed how much attention we pay to naming our babies?

I saw this in the Bible: God established the four seasons after the flood

I saw this in the pen: Training involves four seasons

Gen 1:14 "God spoke: "Lights! Come out! Shine in Heaven's sky! Separate Day from Night. Mark seasons and days and years.""

I've always wondered what Adam thought of the four seasons that God established after the flood. The Bible says Adam was told by God to tend the garden and care for it, so I guess he would have been the first to understand what season to plant and what season would be the harvest.

In the round pen, I also saw seasons. Now the seasons of training are slightly difference then the seasons we attach to weather and time of the year. Seasons with a horse comes in levels of training and understanding. The fit is you can't change that natural progression and you can't get the seasons out of order without creating a mess. Learning the seasons helps us keep on track in life. It gives us a predictable change that encourages creation.

I saw this in the Bible: God gave us authority over livestock.

I saw this in the pen: The trainer is always in charge of the horse

Isa. 32:20 "But you will enjoy a blessed life, planting well-watered fields and gardens, with your farm animals grazing freely."

Gen 1:28 "God blessed them: "Prosper! Reproduce! Fill Earth! Take charge! Be

responsible for fish in the sea and birds in the air, for every living thing that moves on

the face of Earth."

God certainly set the stage for all of us to become successful farmers and ranchers. His Word gave us authority over livestock, He gave us seasons, and He gave us lessons on planting, the need to water, and the harvest. God even extends His insight to fishermen, and other endeavors. But God, in the end, spends more time with farmers and ranchers than any other trade.

In the round pen, it's always been important that the trainer and the horse fully understand who's in charge right from the get-go. Authority is not meant to be a measure of instilling fear or punishment that's extreme. Authority becomes the standard by which all new information will be gained. You are the boss.

Having established that, here's al ittle hint from years of training horses: some lessons are best learned by the horse for the horse. The horse will dish out just the right amount of understanding if you don't interfere to himself.

I saw this in the Bible: God is not a problem solver.
God creates new life.

I saw this in the pen: I'm not there to problem solve
- I'm there to create

Eph. 2:10 "No, we neither make nor save ourselves. God does both the making and saving. He creates each of us by Christ Jesus to join Him in the work He does, the good work He has gotten ready for us to do, work we had better be doing."

It's a mistake if you think that God is here to give you something or to solve your problems. God is in the business of making and saving. The cycle of always creating never stops in our lives. It's how we grow in Christ. Father God extends an open door policy for all of us to be in relationship with Him in the plans and work He does in our lives. There is only one simple notion to being in God's plan: don't you walk out of the room.

The horse in the round pen, if left alone, won't be motivated to learn anything. He will wander around aimlessly searching for what he doesn't even know. In the round pen, you have to stay engaged in the relationship and set the stage for learning. In the end, you'll see the fruit of your creation.

The classic mistake that people make in this culture is to change "words" that they find in the Bible to take on new meaning that suits their purpose. Another classic mistake is to take one verse out of a chapter and hang onto it like it was all there was. Take the time to read 10 verses back and 10 verses forward and that one Scripture may well take on a whole different meaning.

In this media-driven world, there is no excuse for not understanding the Word. E-Sword is a free app that will supply you with all sorts of comparisons and commentary. Use this valueable tool and you'll be surprised how quickly you can gain knowledge.

Chapter 15
Daily Bread

I still believe that every day I pray, "Give Us This Day Our Daily Bread," I'm not going to starve to death. That simple prayer for me contains more "child-like faith" than anything I can think of.

There is one or two books that I think belong in your home. God's Promises is $1.99 at Wal-Mart. The ISBN is 978-1-55748-105-4; it contains all the key verses you need for most anything that comes up. If you don't have copies of Psalms 91 by Peggy Joyce Ruth, make sure you ask Saint Rhonda to get you the books off my office shelf. Of course, it bears witness that Escape From the Southern Comfort Christian Society will show you exactly what happened when I gave my life over to Christ.

Reading may not be your favorite pastime, but don't stop getting in the Word over reading. Get the CD's and the DVD's that are free.

I pray over my entire family that God richly bless each and every one of you. I always pray Psalms 91, our Psalm of protection, over all of you. Lastly, know that I love each of you beyond your understanding. God speed.

Chapter 16
Afraid To Die

After years of embattlement over LTCI (Long Term Chronic Illness), I had become more than a little disenchanted with non-Christian doctors. I began to pray, "Father God, Your Word says, Ask and ye shall receive." And you fully understand that I remain almost embattled with all these different doctors. Every time I would mention something about my faith or that I was already healed, they would get that disapproving smile going and then typically went south in a hurry.

Lo and behold, I ended up getting a new primary physician. Within a very short period of time, we both discovered a love for Jesus that we had in common. After more than a year, I truly had total trust in having my new Christian Doctor help manage my medical conditions. I also discovered two lung doctors who were Christians, a Heart Doctor, and a VA doctor. I not only had my prayers answered; I believe I was overly blessed with the best of anointed care.

It was my Christian doctor that said, "I'm here to entertain you, God's here to heal you." Another Christian doctor pointed out that they were in relationship with me to bring about all their medical expertise to help control the symptoms. They, too, were very clear that God does the healing and they do what the Father has anointed them to do. It was that doctor that certainly made living with COPD smoother.

In the end, I had to admit some of the truths that I was living with concerning COPD. For starters, I had struggled during the years to keep from dying over and over. I can't tell you how many times I was sure that the end was upon me. Call it what you may, there is a sheer sense of panic when you can't breathe. You do feel like you're drowning.

I was afraid to die. I prayed, I searched the Scriptures, I talked to pastors, and I was even open and honest with Saint Rhonda. Spiritually I thought I was in fine shape; it was the flesh that kept me going sideways.

One day, I was reading some timeline posts on Facebook and I came across this post that said on its heading: "Death ~ What a Wonderful Way to Explain It." I later found the source; Catholic Study Fellowship, February 8, 2014.

This is that posting, and I quote:

"A sick man turned to his doctor as he was preparing to leave the examination room and said, "Doctor, I'm afraid to die. Tell me what lies on the other side." Very quickly, the doctor said, "I don't know...."

'You don't know? You're a Christian man, and don't know what's on the other side?" The doctor was holding the handle of the door, and from the other side came a sound of scratching and whining. And as he opened the door, a dog sprang into the room and leaped on him with an eager show of gladness.

Turning to the patient, the doctor said, "Did you notice my dog? He's never been in this room before. He didn't know what was inside. He knew nothing except that his master was here, and when the door opened, he sprang in without fear. I know little of what is on the other side of death, but I do know one thing …

I know my Master is there and that is enough."

Again, it's near the end of March, 2014 and I am about to receive another blow to the gut. I'm about to be discharged at Medical City Hospital in Dallas when our renowned Pulmonary Team member Dr. Motta steps into our room with the final reports from the CT Scan, the TEE, and X-rays. He's about to deliver his "summary," prior to discharge instructions.

Of course by now, Dr. Motta and I have had one or two "Mexican standoffs," to establish the precise mythology we will use to bring information to each other. We are two peas in a pod over not wasting words, effort, and false insinuations. What we have learned about each other is our need to bring our "issues," to the surface and have them dealt with honestly. We do not play "gloss over."

This is an attempt to paraphrase Doctor Motta's speech that evening: "Jay, based on the current records, our history of testing, all the procedures we have completed and analysis feedback, you are a victim of Asbestos contact, which has resulted in both of your lungs being permanently damaged. At this time, you have significant scarring of both lung bottoms on both sides, which has rendered them useless and failed. You operate only with the capacity left in the left and right upper lung lobes.

Your history indicates that this initial contact with Asbestos occurred during your active duty in the US Navy, starting in year 1961, through your active duty and return in September 1964. Additionally, your work history with Ingersol Rand Co for the next 5 plus years results in continued daily exposure to Asbestos.

I recommend you contact the US Navy and apply for a change in status in your disability. I would also advise you to engage counsel in regards to the Ingersoll Rand case. This is your opportunity to provide for your family after you have gone.

I will provide you with a letter stating this diagnosis of Asbestosis of the lungs and obtain the records they may need to support the findings.

He did talk a little about Mesothelioma, the lung cancer part of Asbestosis disease. There is a 8% chance I will contact that cancer during this Stage 4 COPD timeline.

The discussion sort of trailed off leaving Saint Rhonda and I in a semi-state of shock. We're pretty used to negative medical reports, although the largest percentage of time, I seem to manage good numbers.

Perhaps it was the long-term fear of the unknown that became the short time reality of what I had just been told. I must say, the term "black lung," that was often used when I lived in Painted Post, the upstate New York town, that houses Ingersoll Rand, came to mind quickly. Here in Texas, they were ok with just saying you have Asbestosis of the Lungs. Of course, just like you I've seen a hundred of those "hammer down attorney," ads that talk about settlements for victims of Mesothelioma. To a degree, I'm surprised I didn't contract the cancer end of that stick. I do know I have such a distrust of TV attorney ads that I would not call them.

Over the years, I had settled into a think stream that allowed me to come down to the casket in a gentle sort of way. It was sort of like the long way around. In the long way around, you get to kid yourself that we really don't know when death will occur. That's true, we don't - but we like the feeling of being able to hedge the bet. It was sort of a plan to back door myself into the casket of death without really facing it. However, this was different, I'm hearing the phrase Asbestosis lungs. Hearing Asbestosis tore that veil all to shreds. Asbestosis was associated, in my mind, with harshness, violence, tormented death scenes, and unbearable pain.

I had a friend, David, who I had witnessed death with during his last four weeks on earth. He had cancer and I think COPD and it hit him like a freight train. This guy and his wife were just the perfect couple one likes to hang with. They were great bowlers, way above average, loved tournaments, loved to travel, and were also so happy. He was a State Inspector for the highway department. She worked in a Peterbilt truck factory over in Denton, building semi-tractor trailer trucks.

Bam, right out of the clear blue sky, David went from total health to total chaos in his earth suit. His entire body just bolted sideways on him, and neither he nor his medical team had any control over the piercing bouts of system lost, and the intense, ongoing pain. This was like a man consumed with live fires burning everywhere in his body.

They quickly set up a hospital bed in his living room and transferred him with a truck load of drugs designed to knock him senseless over the pain for some needed relief. David had this dog, this short legged, yappy, Mexican type dog that was darn sure his buddy. They had this long term relationship established and when David was brought home, the dog took over. He climbed up by David in the bed and watch guarded over his master like a pit bull. One had to approach David with some caution.

Meanwhile, I'm stuck in this bed in Medical City - wanting to go home - and all my mind is focused on is David. I really am starting to grasp how we develop fear in our lives. The devil has somehow got me focused on David's event during his last days and keeps me thinking that's going to be you. If I listen to that I've certainly forgot "but God."

I push the negative stuff out of the way with the help of Father just long enough to renew and refocus on what comes next.

Now I'm into another battle - the fear of being that individual that everyone talks about the minute they get involved in a "cash settlement," or the change of disability status that ends up giving them something they may or may not deserve.

I'm stunned at the rapid fire responses my brain seems to want to kick up. It's overloaded on the flight or fight mode. Once again I grasp at the moment to spill this latest fear back out to Dr. Motta.

In a very quick straight forward manner, he set me straight. "You paid for that with your service, you didn't knowingly work in the Rand just so you could get Asbestosis. You, my friend, have an obligation to receive what is justified for your case and that financial package will ensure your family's future after you're gone." He ended with "You need to get busy and take care of this."

Ok, that helped. The doctor has directed me to do something; who's to fight with your doctor? Not me.

As we go home, we start talking about what I need or may need in the near future to help manage this end lifestyle. We describe a list; not a wish list, just a list. We start with getting my status changed from non-service connected disability to service-connected disability. We've heard that I could get help with the conversion cost of owning a van set up with a side ramp and passenger loading dock. That cost is somewhere around $18,000 to $25,000, from what we are hearing. Then you still are left with paying for a $30,000 dollar van; give or take. Then I remember the last vet up the street that we worked for got a new Toyota Van with a ramp and hand controls and he said it was in the low $70,000 dollar range. .He told me his personal outlay was $17,000 and the VA gave him an allowance amount for the conversion and an allowance towards purchase of the van.

When we arrived home, I went into the offices and drafted a letter to my local VA doctor here at the Sherman Clinic inquiring as to what I had to do to process a change order for disability. As I glanced at the appointments for the rest of the week, I see I'm to go to the Dallas VA hospital and get re-evaluated by Shirley the next morning. I fired off a fax copy of the letter to the local doctor to her fax machine, just so she would know what's going on. I see Rhonda is in search of a local attorney. I call our normal attorney office and get a referral. I call this attorney, Benjamin Baker's office, and they end up setting a time for him to come to our home to talk to us. That struck me as odd.

Then the VA lady called and switched my appointment from Thursday to Friday. Then I called the attorney, as he allowed he could come in the morning, that Thursday. Believe it or not, it all worked out.

The attorney explains that Ingersoll Rand already acknowledges the claims and in fact they had settled over 208,000 claims over the last quarter century, with settlements totaling $308 million. Currently, they have added funds to bring their kitty up to $755 million available for settlement now and in the future up to year 2053.

He took an application out and we spent over an hour filling in the blanks. The attorney ended up saying, "I don't know how much or when you will receive your settlement; but you will receive one." Rhonda asked, "Guess on the time line." He replied, "Less than a year."

I was a parts chaser, for gathering and tracking all the components that it takes to build a compressor. My job each day was to locate, track, and bring together a large number of sub assembly products into the final stages of finished and ready to ship. Nothing was out of my reach, not buildings, not materials, and certainly not asbestos. It was on the gaskets I looked at, it was on the wrappings used on pipe systems, it was in the walls, it was everywhere. Any time I drove up the block to find a new casting being made and entered into the foundry, the exposure was way over the top. Many men who worked in the factory for years at that building died from lung related disease.

At that point, we concluded our meeting and signed a Contingent Fee Contract with Attorney Baker to represent us.

We certainly were off and running. Our next move was to track and get all the report findings from all the test, CT scans, X-rays, Tee, you name it from day one of the search for what had attacked my lungs. That started in late November and early December 2008 out of Dr. Millman's office. That first shadow on that in-house x-ray film pushed me to Advanced Medical Imaging to Texas Oncology at the Paris Regional Cancer Center to Wilson and Jones Hospital in January, 2009 for the lung surgery. Then we moved on to UT Southwestern Medical Center's Pulmonary Specialty Clinic in Dallas. Then all the scans, x-rays etc. that came from Medical City Hospital. That included tests ordered from Dr. Julette Wait's group, Dr. Richard W Snyder II the Pacemaker surgeon, Dr. Lampe the Electrophysiology guy, and Dr. Lopez in Denison. Finally, the other test came from my local heart doctor, Dr. Winston Marshall at TMC.

I called, she called, and we all called and the reports started coming in fast. What really took us by surprise as we read and reviewed all these findings was one of the early attempts to find out what the spots were acknowledged in their conclusion. They said, "It was related to asbestos contact resulting in lung asbestosis." In fact, we now know someone pinpointed it almost five years ago and nobody jumped on it. Strange.

2008 Paris Oncology in the PET scan noted Asbestos Related pleural disease evidence. Somehow that never got mentioned to us.

This much we always know - forget that looking in the rear view mirror. If's, can's, and would-have-been don't count.

The only reason that above statement of finding alerts anyone is because it doesn't fit our own designed cookie mold. If someone operates outside the box, then we are quick to run the blame game up.

What if I saw this as part of God's plan to allow me to live the past five years and not worry about dying with Asbestos lungs. That only leaves me all in with thanksgiving for the blessed break in stress. Thank you Jesus for giving me the grace I didn't know I needed. If you think about it, God's plan erased that fear that certainly was there.

I think we certainly need to pay attention to the way Jesus does things. God's plans are so plain, so creative, so full of life that we often just act dumber than a jar of dirt. Really, don't get defensive - we may all be in the box but to think we are all the brightest color is over stepping our pay rate for sure.

I truly believe that the slowing down process that our culture likes to pin on the backs of senior citizen is in reality a re-focus gift sent to each of us by God so that we don't miss out on the joys of this whole earth mother news before we go to heaven.

This morning, I was glued to my water fountain and mesmerized by the waters of life that flow from the top rock all the way to the bottom of the pond. I saw light in the water, it was coolness. I saw and heard the gentle tapping of a million water drops following God's plan for their lives. Jesus said, I will give you …. And there it was, in all its glory.

I stared at a great-grandbaby on Facebook this afternoon and fell in love with my own offspring, Ms. Harper. I saw Jesus manifest Himself through us as a family unit, strong and proud to serve Him. I realized that I have laid the pathway for Ms. Harper but Ms. Harper will provide the story. On earth, I find it almost impossible to gather my family to my side, but I see clearly now the other side where we come together.

After hours, days, weeks, and months of reading the word, reading other healing books, listening to Pastor Duane's tapes, and formulating my own views, I've found someone better than me to tell you my lasting thoughts.

Deborah Smith Pegues wrote a book Emergency Prayers. God's help in your Time of Need. I found one of those prayers and have reworked it to fit me. It's not an emergency prayer in my world - it's simply the truth.

Father God, I want to take the time to pray with You about this life -threatening illness that my earth suit has. The devil, the most evil thing I've ever dealt with has come to steal, kill, and destroy me. But I trust in your Word which says You have come that I may have life, and have it to the full (John 10;10) Even though the doctor's report is negative, I know that You have the last word regarding my life. You saw me before I was born. Every day of my life was recorded in Your book. Every moment was laid out before a single day had passed. (Psalms 139:16)

Forgive me, Father for any door I may have opened for this sickness by not being a good steward of my health. Surround me with Your tender mercies so I may live (Psalms 119:77). Raise me up as a testimony of Your great healing power. You are the same miracle working God yesterday, today, and forever (Hebrews 13:8)

I take authority over every malfunctioning part of my body. I command each one to be made whole. I decree that I will not die before my appointed time, but will live to tell what You have done (Psalm118:17). Therefore I say on the authority of Your Word, that with the stripes of Jesus, I am healed (Isaiah 53:5). In the name of Jesus I pray. Amen

At the end of life, as I die to live, I am drawn to the words of my oldest daughter who was planted in the garden with a heart so large it nearly doesn't fit her wonderful body. Tammy said to me, "Dad, God will keep you in His care. My thoughts and prayers are with you each and every day. I love you, Tammy. Here's your verse: He answered their prayers because they trusted in Him, 1 Chronicles 5:20 NIV.

Till we meet again, keep your eyes fixed on the external trail to heaven, I'll be waiting.

Holy Cow ~ Can You Believe That   I overheard one of the grandkids tell the other one that asked the question, "You can, if Popeye said so." You just gotta love the Zackman from West Texas.

Chapter 17

God Speaks Back

When Popeye thought he had finished this book, I still had some lessons for him to learn; this is Popeye's version of what I said to him before the final page was printed. A word from Father God.

Today you joined hundreds of people who celebrated Ms. Pete's life on earth. I realize it was very hard for you, yet I'm glad you realize that Ms. Pete is right here with me and we're in the middle of a giant celebration. Eugene H. Peterson's translation of the last two verses of Psalms 91 was spot on. We are indeed hosting a party and Ms. Pete is having the time of her "new life." My Word was exactly what you saw and experienced during those last days and hours while Ms. Pete was on earth.

I took the opportunity to bring other friends to Ms. Pete's bedside. There were some unfinished business in that room and by My grace, I brought some of those relationships back for a final good-bye. I'm also glad to see that you were aware of Ms. Pete's appointed time, even when you didn't know the exact hour.

Those last days and last weeks when you and Ms. Pete didn't fully understand why or what was going on, I want you to know that I was pleased you found and held on to that cornerstone verse in Proverbs. Instead of both of you trying to fully understand, you did indeed acknowledge Father God. This is a key word for all your readers. All these God Stories from the Back of the Herd point to one verse of major importance. It is the key to peace in the end.

I also noticed you and Ms. Pete stood on My promises. You did my foundation for you from beginning of time and as you experienced that, you fully rely on God with no reserve. At last you have found how much I love you. As you both released your lives and your care fully into My arms, I could complete what the Father told me to do.

As you close your book, Popeye, make sure you tell you readers this was and is available to them, too. That's the final message from Me and you at the Back of the Herd; Ask, and it shall be given you; seek, and ye shall find; knock, and it shall be opened unto you. My promise, My words for everyone as I inspired the author of Matthew 7:7 to write.

I am pleased with you, My faithful servant. I thank you for making sure that Father God has been put on stage for all the world to see.

The end.

The Back Of The Herd tells their God Stories one last time. Here's their opportunity to get the message of God through to their children and grandchildren. If not now perhaps a day will come in the future where lives will be changed.

Popeye Harnish

The Word says: "It is the spirit that quickeneth; the flesh profiteth nothing; the words what I speak unto you, they are spirit, and they are life" John 6:63

Popeye Harnish holds degrees in Human Services, Clinical Social Work, and Research Sociology from Corning College, University of Texas Arlington. Popeye is married to Rhonda L Harnish and Oct 21 will celebrate their 26th year of marriage. They are a blended family of 7 children and 19 grandchildren.

Jon Penton Photography contributed the pictures.

Published, Produced, & Distributed by

Island Entertainment Media

Get your book, manuscript or audiobook produced for
FREE today!

www.islandentertainmentmedia.com

Email:

IslandEntertainmentMedia@gmail.com

www.ingramcontent.com/pod-product-compliance
Lightning Source LLC
Chambersburg PA
CBHW060925040426
42445CB00011B/794